HIGH P

The Covid-19 pandemic, with its resulting lockdowns and significant changes to ways of working, has provided the opportunity to redefine the potential role that health and wellbeing can play within organisations.

Empowering employees to work in ways that optimise their performance, acknowledging both personal and work demands, has created a new work paradigm that had previously not been considered. All savvy organisations will take this as a point in time to rethink business and HR practice, for the benefits of employees and employers. Written by the Head of Associate Health and Wellbeing (Europe) at Mars Incorporated, Dr Monika Misra, and world-renowned expert on wellbeing in organisations, Sir Cary Cooper, the book provides clear evidence of what worked well during the Covid-19 pandemic that we can learn from and embed today, to enable individuals and organisations to thrive. Basing recommendations on a robust evidence base and through real-life practices within organisations, they provide a framework for a four-level response at organisational, team, management and individual levels.

This book will provide an essential resource to stimulate company leaders, managers and HR, to rethink and reframe new approaches that enhance employee wellbeing, engagement and performance.

Dr Monika Misra, Head of Associate Health and Wellbeing (Europe), Mars Incorporated.

Sir Cary Cooper, CBE, 50th Anniversary Professor of Organizational Psychology and Health, Alliance Manchester Business School, University of Manchester.

HEALTHY HIGH PERFORMANCE

UNLOCKING BUSINESS SUCCESS THROUGH EMPLOYEE WELLBEING

Dr Monika Misra and Sir Cary Cooper

LONDON AND NEW YORK

Designed cover image: Getty Images

First published 2025
by Routledge
4 Park Square, Milton Park, Abingdon, Oxon OX14 4RN

and by Routledge
605 Third Avenue, New York, NY 10158

Routledge is an imprint of the Taylor & Francis Group, an informa business

© 2025 Monika Misra and Cary Cooper

British Library Cataloguing-in-Publication Data
A catalogue record for this book is available from the British Library

Library of Congress Cataloging-in-Publication Data
Names: Misra, Monika, author. | Cooper, Cary L., author.
Title: Healthy high performance : unlocking business success through employee wellbeing / Cary Cooper and Monika Misra.
Description: Abingdon, Oxon ; New York, NY : Routledge, 2025. | Includes bibliographical references and index.
Identifiers: LCCN 2024032266 (print) | LCCN 2024032267 (ebook) | ISBN 9780367645335 (hardback) | ISBN 9780367645342 (paperback) | ISBN 9781003124979 (ebook)
Subjects: LCSH: Industrial hygiene. | Employee health promotion. | Performance. | Personnel management.
Classification: LCC HD7261 . M547 2025 (print) | LCC HD7261 (ebook) | DDC 658.3/8--dc23/eng/20240822
LC record available at https://lccn.loc.gov/2024032266
LC ebook record available at https://lccn.loc.gov/2024032267

ISBN: 978-0-367-64533-5 (hbk)
ISBN: 978-0-367-64534-2 (pbk)
ISBN: 978-1-003-12497-9 (ebk)

DOI: 10.4324/9781003124979

Typeset in Bembo
by SPi Technologies India Pvt Ltd (Straive)

CONTENTS

ACKNOWLEDGEMENTS

With gratitude to my father and mother, Kuldev Rai Misra and Nalini Sushma Misra, for their devotion to the task of helping my brother and I become the best that we can be. Their unconditional love has been a constant support, and through their example, they have shown me the value of diligence, integrity and compassion at work. The insights I gained during my childhood, from listening to their work experiences were invaluable and I had little appreciation of how universal these themes were, not only at the time but for decades to come.

To Pardip, my husband. Thank you for your support to work on this book. Special thanks to my rockstar sons, Paras and Dev, who took full advantage of their free rein whenever I sat down to work on the book!

With appreciation to my mentors and coaches, past and present: Professor Wendy Reid, Mr Adam Lewis, Dr Adrian Chojnacki, Dr Robert Carr, Dr Paul Litchfield, Dr Richard Heron, Dr David Roomes, Susan Cruse, Kris Webb, Gerard Hussey, Lynn Hawkins, Dr Alasdair Emslie, Dr Jonathan Spencer, Dr John Sterland, Linda Renall, Dr Sally Bonneywell, Dr Cathie Mackay, Anita Kidgell, Anne Welsh and Adrian Machon, for your guidance, encouragement and inspiration.

To all those whom I had the pleasure of leading at GlaxoSmithKline, thank you for allowing me the opportunity to experiment, particularly for accepting my epic failures, with understanding and forgiveness. Thank you to my past colleagues, Dr Ashish Jain, Dr Arif Jiwany,

Dr David Siebens, and Dr Phil Ryan. Each one of you became my anchor, teaching me the importance of a strong peer network.

To all my friends at GlaxoSmithKline, thank you for being there. To my new friends at Mars Incorporated, especially Cathryn Gunther, for being a leader I trust, admire and respect. Thank you for your warm welcome, for believing in me and for the immense fun are we having. Your enthusiasm to see this book finished gave me the motivation to get it over the line!

Caren Kenney, I am immensely grateful to you for taking a chance on me, for creating opportunities that have allowed me to continue to follow my passion to support leaders and organisations.

With thanks to my dear friend Priya Kaura, for continuing to nag me to get the book out! To Andrew Parsons, for your generosity in sharing book-writing tips. To my executive coach training buddy, Katarina Kozul, for your ever-present cheerleading and to Rachel Power, for your excitement and infectious high energy.

We would like to acknowledge content suggestions from the following, which have undoubtedly enhanced the value and relevance to the reader: Dr Paul Litchfield, Dr Richard Heron, Susan Cruse, Michael Cole-Fontayn, Richard Pamenter, Humaira Serajuddin and Simon Gunson.

We thank the following for their contribution to the content in this book: Dr Paul Litchfield, Dr Richard Heron, Dr Richard Caddis, Bruce Greenhalgh, Dr Anne De Bono, Andy Rhodes, Dr Ian Hesketh, Professor John Harrison, Deborah Lee, Dr Nick Davison, Dr Samantha Philips, Jennifer Gardner, Zoe Garnett, Angela Raynor, David Fox, Jamie Broadley, Finau Vucago, Kym Bancroft, Professor Ira Madan, Dr Danielle Lamb, Dr Serufusa Sekidde, David Gordon, Dr Tracey Leghorn, Natalie Sáenz, Rhianwen Condron, Ruth Pott, and Ryan Hopkins. Thank you Jennifer Gardner, for connecting us to key contributors from the NHS.

Dr Lina Siegl, thank you for your magic referencing.

To Rajen Yadav. Your illustration design genius has brought the content alive in the most powerful ways!

THE OPPORTUNITY
Employee health and wellbeing is a strategic enabler of business success

Key messages

1. Investment in workforce wellbeing has shifted from being optional, to essential, with strong alignment to the Corporate Social Responsibility (CSR) and Environment, Social and Governance (ESG) agendas. Investors are beginning to understand the effect that human capital management has on financial performance, business sustainability and success.

2. Covid-19 emphasised the importance of demonstrating care for employees, through focussing on employee health and wellbeing, and the resulting positive consequences on business continuity and success.

3. There is a direct link between employee engagement and productivity. One mechanism by which increasing engagement boosts productivity is through enhancing employee health and wellbeing. Efforts made to enhance employee engagement will only be successful if consideration and commitment is made to nurturing employee psychological wellbeing, which is individualistic. Supporting employees to minimise their health risks and optimise their health and wellbeing not only reduces the prevalence of sickness absence and presenteeism associated with poor health but also increases performance by enabling employees and organisations to thrive.

4. Investment in workforce health and wellbeing is not in opposition to the delivery of business priorities but rather an enabler of business success, through positively impacting individual-, leader-, team-, and organisational-level outcomes.

DOI: 10.4324/9781003124979-1

5. Beyond getting the basics of health and safety right, identifying and addressing the root causes of workplace stress at individual and organisational levels, could have the greatest impact on engagement and business outcomes.
6. Prioritising employee health and wellbeing plays a critical role in attracting and retaining talent, and thereby offering a competitive advantage.

INTRODUCTION

Various events of the recent past, including COVID-19, the cost-of-living crisis and geopolitical conflicts, have impacted us all and made uncertainty a norm. To help employees navigate these uncertainties, workplaces are more than ever focussing on supporting positive health and wellbeing, with demonstrable impact on engagement, productivity and, ultimately, business success.

Wellbeing mediates the relationship between engagement and productivity. Let's explore this further.

EMPLOYEE ENGAGEMENT

Origins

The concept of employee engagement has come to the fore relatively recently. Kahn introduced the term as "the harnessing of organization members' selves to their work roles. More specifically, when engaged, people employ and express themselves physically, cognitively, and emotionally during role performances" (Kahn, 1990).

According to Schaufeli and Bakker (2004), work engagement captures an enduring, positive and fulfilling affective-cognitive state of mind at work, characterised by vigour, dedication and absorption. Vigour refers to a high level of positive energy at work and willingness to invest one's efforts in the job, even in the face of difficulties. Dedication is characterised by inspiration, sense of significance and enthusiasm. Absorption captures employees' full concentration. Within this context, engagement could be deemed the antithesis of burnout (Maslach & Leiter, 1997).

Many studies have suggested measures to enhance employee engagement and significant investment has been, and still is, being made in this regard. For instance, in their model, Bakker and Demerouti (2008) included job resources (e.g., autonomy and performance feedback) and personal resources (e.g., self-efficacy and optimism) as antecedents of work engagement, which lead to improved performance. They found that job resources enhance engagement, especially when job demands are high (Bakker et al., 2007). A fundamental role of the line manager is to reflect upon and identify (with inputs from individuals within their team) what specific support would make a difference to each individual, and the team as a whole, in relation to their engagement. A reflective question for managers is 'What more do I need to do to support my team's health and wellbeing?' While managers play a big role in this, it is important to acknowledge that there is joint accountability, and employees must figure out 'What do I need to do to support my health and wellbeing?'

The term 'engagement' is being used less frequently in the workplace, being replaced by more contemporaneous terms such as a 'thriving' or 'energised' workforce, which have similar sentiments and meanings.

The business case for engagement

Productivity growth has been falling in the UK for several decades since a peak in the 1960s, and has been particularly weak since the 2008 financial crisis (Jackson, 2019).

Extensive research has demonstrated several positive effects of improving employee engagement, and, therefore, there has been a drive throughout many companies, over the past decade, to focus on enhancing employee engagement. These benefits have been observed across multiple levels.

Organisational impact

A study on firefighters found a strong relationship between engagement and performance, where engagement was found to be more predictive of task performance than intrinsic motivation, job involvement and job satisfaction (Rich et al., 2010).

Within public and private organisations, engagement has been found to correlate with high levels of task performance, creativity and organisational citizenship behaviour (Bakker, 2014) and positive customer interaction (Chalofsky, 2010). In order to thrive in today's world, many companies need and value creativity. As a result of increasing openness to new experiences, engaged workers have more creative ideas and are more likely to innovate and be entrepreneurial (Gawke et al., 2017).

Among police officers, engagement has been found to harness organisational commitment (Richardsen et al., 2006). In today's post-pandemic world, with the reality of 'mass resignation' and a hot labour market, staff retention is a priority for employers, to avoid the challenges of staff turnover and to retain key talent.

For readers interested in the bottom line, engaged workers, through the enhanced job and personal resources described above, yield better financial results (Xanthopoulou et al., 2009).

Team impact

Teamwork engagement is defined as a shared, positive and fulfilling, motivational emergent state of work-related wellbeing (Costa et al., 2014). Teamwork engagement correlates positively with team performance, whereby discussing ideas positively influences the transformation of the team's level of engagement, in the form of energy and enthusiasm, into objective performance (Costa et al., 2015). The manager has a role to play in creating the environment of trust to enable these kinds of open discussions to take place (see Chapter 3 on the role of the manager in creating a (psychologically) safe working environment).

Engaged workers are inclined to help their colleagues if needed (Halbesleben & Wheeler 2008). As observed in the firefighter study above (Rich et al., 2010), employees reporting higher levels of engagement also reported being more friendly, courteous, and helpful towards colleagues and thereby experienced more positive, individual affective states, which subsequently influenced their overall performance.

Individual impact

Among police officers, engagement has been found to harness not only organisational commitment but also self-efficacy (Richardsen et al., 2006). Engagement is good for our health. Employees who report higher levels of engagement are more likely to report lower levels of emotional exhaustion and higher levels of personal accomplishment with their work, as well as increased levels of psychological wellbeing (Shuck & Reio, 2014), all of which reduce the likelihood of conditions such as burnout.

How engaged are we globally?

Despite this clear business case and greater employer attention on enhancing engagement, according to Gallup's State of the Global Workplace report, 2023, low engagement is costing the global economy $8.8 trillion, which is 9% of global GDP. In 2022, only 23% of the world's employees identified themselves as being engaged (finding work meaningful, feeling connected, taking ownership for their performance and going the extra mile); however, the majority (59%) were not engaged (quietly quitting, putting in minimal effort, psychologically disconnected from their employer and at risk of burnout and stress) and 18% were actively disengaged (organisational harm caused through actions resulting from severed trust). According to the survey, a whopping 51% of employees are actively seeking alternative employment (Gallup, 2023). A similar finding was captured though a survey conducted by the UK's Chartered Institute for Personnel and Development (CIPD), the professional body for human resources (HR), learning and development (L&D), organisation development (OD) and all people professionals, with more than 160,000 members globally and a growing community using its research, insights and learning. CIPD's Good Work Index 2023, which surveyed approximately 5000 UK workers, found that only about a quarter of workers feel full of energy at work (Young, 2023).

Despite many organisations making significant investments to enhance employee engagement, why has the dial has not shifted significantly?

A theory proposed by Robertson et al. is that most definitions of engagement are *organisation-focused* with little regard for what individuals deem important, and any attempts to enhance employee engagement will thus achieve only limited success if they concentrate narrowly on employee commitment and citizenship, without seeking to nurture *employee psychological wellbeing*, which, being more employee-focused, is likely to be more important to employees (Robertson & Cooper, 2010). In line with this, the majority of employees, who were not engaged in the Gallup survey, felt that the areas that would make the biggest difference were improving culture or engagement, pay and benefits and wellbeing. Further evidence of overlap between engagement and employee wellbeing comes from an NHS study. After surveying 10,000 NHS employees in Great Britain, the Institute of Employment Studies highlights that the key driver of employee engagement is a sense of *feeling valued and involved*, which has components such as involvement in decision-making, the extent to which employees feel able to voice their ideas, the opportunities employees have to develop in their jobs and the extent to which the organisation is concerned for *employees' health and wellbeing* (Robinson et al., 2004). Not only does employee health and wellbeing positively influence worker engagement, low employee wellbeing has been shown to negatively impact work behaviour and performance (Sonnentag, 2015) and incurs large costs (Cooper & Dewe, 2008). Leaders, therefore, must consider the opportunity to enhance business success through prioritising the health and wellbeing of their employees.

WELLBEING

Wellbeing means different things to different people and there appears to be a lack of consensus around a single definition of wellbeing. It can be limited to physical and mental health or widened to encompass the various aspects of life satisfaction. For instance, wellbeing is defined by the Oxford English Dictionary as "the state of being comfortable, healthy, or happy". Self-Determination Theory suggests that we have three intrinsic psychological needs that, when satisfied, lead to optimal wellbeing: autonomy, relatedness, and competence. In the work context, autonomy refers to the feeling of being in control of one's work environment and feeling that one has a sense of volition and choice. Relatedness refers to the perception that one can form quality relationships at work. Competence refers to one's ability to experience a sense of efficacy or mastery at work (Ryan & Deci, 2000). This timeless model is relevant in any work setting, with the three dimensions being invaluable in explaining why some employees thrive and others struggle and for use as a discussion guide for managers (exploring the three areas with their team) and for personal reflection on ways they can better engage their team members. Seligman formed his model of psychological wellbeing on the basis that, in addition to engagement, the other four core constituents of psychological wellbeing that support individuals to flourish are: positive emotion, relationships, meaning and achievement (abbreviated to PERMA) (Seligman, 2011). These five constituents include both *eudaimonic* and *hedonic* components. 'Hedonic' wellbeing focuses on the "feeling" component of wellbeing (e.g. enjoyment and satisfaction) whereas 'eudaimonic' wellbeing focuses on the "thinking" component of wellbeing (e.g. meaning, value and fulfilment) (Ryff & Keyes, 1995). We all need both hedonia and eudaimonia to flourish (Turban & Yan, 2016) and organisations should focus on both of these complementary aspects of wellbeing, i.e., creating an environment that fosters personal growth, a sense of purpose and a feeling of social significance, in addition to hedonic happiness.

The UK the Office for National Statistics (ONS) (the executive office of the UK Statistics Authority, a non-ministerial department which reports directly to the UK Parliament) defines wellbeing as having 10 broad dimensions which have been shown to matter most to people in the UK, as identified through a national debate. These dimensions are: the natural environment, personal wellbeing, our relationships, health, what we do, where we live, personal finance, the economy, education and skills, and governance. Many organisations, such as the UK-based telecommunications company British Telecom, use the comprehensive and evidence-based Whatworks Centre's model of wellbeing, which defines five key drivers of wellbeing. These five areas of subjective wellbeing can be used to underpin organisational health and wellbeing strategy and interventions (see Figure 1.1).

Models serve to ensure a comprehensive and holistic approach to wellbeing that truly enables their employees to thrive.

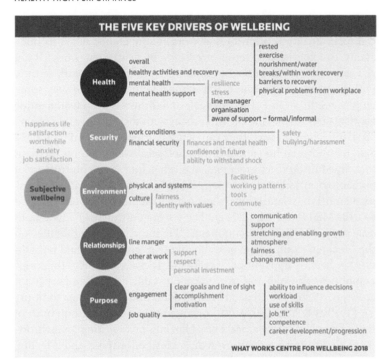

Figure 1.1 The five key drivers of workplace wellbeing

Employee health and wellbeing – The business case

The extent to which an organisation commits to employee health and wellbeing (EH&W) varies hugely, with significant investment at one end. Motivations for this include alignment to company values and mission, attracting and retaining the best talent, boosting employee engagement and productivity and the notion that it is the 'right' thing to do as part of their Corporate Social Responsibility agenda.

There are obvious financial gains in supporting employees to lower their health risks, particularly for organisations based in countries where they fund individual healthcare through insurance schemes, such as in the US. Even where organisations are based in countries where the state funds healthcare, perceptions are starting to change regarding who is responsible for EH&W. While historically this may have been seen as something between the individual and their healthcare system, organisations are becoming increasingly aware of the benefits in supporting their employees to enhance their wellbeing at the individual and organisational level. As a result, they are taking on a greater role in promoting wellbeing and providing means by which employees can optimise their wellbeing. These include access to resources to improve all aspects of wellbeing.

The Environment, Social and Governance (ESG) agenda is gaining significant traction. The 'Social' part of this is increasingly in the spotlight in relation to the role it plays in risk management and business continuity, with investors interested in how employee health and wellbeing impacts human capital management and thus contributes to an organisation's long-term resilience and sustainability (Street et al., 2021).

At the other end of the spectrum, organisational investment in EH&W is perceived as an option or a luxury that is a 'nice to have' in prosperous times, with the EH&W agenda often deprioritised when times get tough. This is the opposite of what is needed to lift the organisation up and out, as the Covid-19 pandemic clearly highlighted. This discretionary relationship with EH&W is usually driven by the lack of understanding of the true value of prioritising employee health and wellbeing.

There are three ways to look at how investment in EH&W contributes to business value.

1. **Minimising the adverse effects of work on health**
   Duty of care, regulatory compliance and reputation

Organisations have historically focussed on minimising employee exposure to physical workplace hazards, like noise or chemical exposure, due to legal obligations that stipulate an employer's duty to protect the health, safety, and welfare of employees, such as the Health and Safety at Work Act 1974, in the UK [Health and Safety at Work etc. Act (1974)]. The visibility of, and objectivity in, diagnosing the manifestations of physical hazards enable occupational health and safety practitioners to identify actions that minimise employee exposure, and conduct health assessments to diagnose health effects at an early stage, seek appropriate medical interventions and advise on modifications or workplace adjustments (the importance of investing in workplace occupational health and wellbeing experts is covered in Chapter 6). This has enabled employers to fulfil their responsibilities under health and safety law and employees to work with the reassurance that there is minimal impact on their health. Preventing illness and injury has been the mainstay of occupational health services, and, consequently, they have focussed on monitoring health regularly to detect early signs of predominantly physical ill health.

Until relatively recently, there was little awareness that work can also have a significant impact on the 'psychological' health of employees and that their psychological health can have consequences on work-ability. Today, organisations are making the shift to focus more on mental wellbeing. This is a result of better control of physical hazard exposure, but also greater awareness that mental health has an equal, if not greater impact on organisational productivity when compared with physical health, and that organisations can play a vital role in helping employees with manage their mental wellbeing. While the causes of poor mental wellbeing are often not work-related, work can adversely affect our physical, and our mental health. A meta-analysis of 228 studies, assessing the effects of ten workplace stressors on four health outcomes, found that job insecurity increases the odds of reporting poor health by about 50%, high job demands raise the odds of having a physician-diagnosed illness by 35%, and long work hours increase mortality by almost 20%. These stark findings reinforce the strong link that exists between our physical and mental health, highlight the relationship between health and the work environment while emphasizing the value of addressing workplace stressors to reduce health costs, improve health outcomes and enhance productivity (Goh et al., 2015). Assessing and supporting employee mental wellbeing is increasingly being incorporated into the requirements of employers under health and safety legislation, for example guidance is available on how to manage work-related stress in the workplace, such as the Stress Management Standards published by Britain's national regulator for workplace health and safety (Health and Safety Executive, n.d.).

One of the most impactful actions line managers and leaders can take to support employee wellbeing is to identify (with the employee) and address the root causes of work stress, at individual and collective levels.

2.   Minimising the adverse effect of poor health on workability and productivity
Sickness absence and presenteeism

Ill-health can influence productivity through both absenteeism and presenteeism. Occupational health services support employees to access the right treatment for their condition in a timely manner, often liaising with medical specialists. Presenteeism occurs when employees choose to attend work when ill, but experience reductions in their performance and productivity on the job due to their health condition. It is a phenomenon in which people are present at work but operating at less than their full capacity.

The greater the number of health risks present for an individual, the higher their rate of self-reported absenteeism and, in particular, presenteeism (Boles et al., 2004). Presenteeism results in significant productivity and financial losses. A study evaluating presenteeism among employees of a large United States health care system, operating in six locations, over a four-year period estimated lost productivity due to poor health and its potential economic burden (Allen et al., 2018). Conditions with the highest estimated daily productivity loss and annual cost per person were chronic back pain, mental illness, general anxiety, migraines or severe headaches, neck pain, and depression. Presenteeism has a greater impact on productivity than absenteeism. Another US-based study found that productivity losses of presenteeism linked to mental health problems were 5.1 times larger than the losses resulting from absenteeism. (Goetzel et al., 2004). This higher prevalence of mental health presenteeism was likely due to the stigma and fear of negative employment consequences and, as a result, presenteeism costs were higher than medical costs in most cases and represented 18% to 60% of overall medical costs. While organisations are starting to make efforts to address presenteeism, more than a third (36%) are not taking any steps according to the 2022 workplace wellbeing CIPD report (CIPD, 2022). Measures to address this include investigating and addressing the causes of presenteeism, and leadership role-modelling positive behaviours, such as not working when unwell, seeking professional support for their health, and taking their full allotted vacation time, to encourage others to do the same.

Improving productivity through enhancing the health and wellbeing of their workforce, needs employers to raise the profile of wellbeing, particularly mental health, and normalise poor mental health, in order to better support those at work as well as off sick (stigma is addressed in Chapter 4).

3. **Optimising wellbeing to enhance performance**
Individual, manager, team and organisational impact

Individual level impact

Creativity, productivity and positive emotion

Creativity is highly sought after by many organisations. It is enhanced by positive emotions. The term 'affect' alludes to our mood or emotion. It is often used to describe the external signs of emotion, as perceived by another person (*Collins Dictionary of Medicine*).

A study on workers in call centres showed that start of workday mood, or mood before calls more generally, affected the productivity of call centre agents such that perceived positive affect after calls related to better quality of work (Rothbard & Wilk, 2011). In addition to work quality, individuals in positive mood states are more cooperative, more helpful, and less aggressive (Isen, & Baron, 1991), which will likely improve productivity in social or collaborative work contexts.

Positive emotion not only feels good but can also develop enhanced states of psychological wellbeing as well as broaden available resources for an individual, thereby contributing to performance (Fredrickson & Joiner, 2002). Frederickson's 'broaden-and-build' theory suggested that positive emotions increase available affective and cognitive resources. For example, a person who experiences joy is more likely to experience flexible, creative, and critical thinking processes than someone who is angry (Fredrickson, 2001). Of particular interest here was the finding that the personal resources accrued by the individual during such moments of positive emotion are enduring, operating like emotional reservoirs that can be drawn on in the future, like a bank account, highlighting the lasting, durable, resilient effect of experiencing positive emotions. Increasing positive emotions at work should be a focus for managers and leaders, through social interactions, team building and opportunities for having fun.

Psychological wellbeing correlates with performance, in that those with higher levels of psychological wellbeing perform better at work than people with lower psychological wellbeing. In fact, wellbeing was a stronger predictor of job performance than job satisfaction (Wright, & Cropanzano, 2000). According to CIPD'S 2021 Good Work Index, which surveyed more than 5000 workers across the UK across different sectors and occupations, showed that workers with higher health and wellbeing scores reported higher task performance (Norris-Green & Gifford, 2021).

Change

Change is certain and constant in the current world of work and dealing positively with change provides an advantage for the employee and employer. Encouragingly, those demonstrating psychological wellbeing are less likely to see ambiguous events as threatening, learn and problem-solve more effectively, are more enthusiastic about change, relate to others more positively and accept change more readily (Cartwright & Cooper, 2008).

Manager level impact

Decision-making and productivity

A study exploring affect at the management level conducted managerial simulations (e.g., running a fictitious production plant) as part of a weekend assessment centre, including a three-hour exercise in which participants must work themselves through a simulated inbox under time pressure, with 21 different decision items. They found that management students with higher levels of positive affect performed better in terms of interpersonal tasks (within-group discussions) and overall decision-making, two key skills needed for managers to be successful and highly valued by staff they manage (Staw & Barsade, 1993). This finding is supported by an increase in self-reported productivity in a study of 75 directors employed in the private and public sectors, where managers with higher levels of positive affect rated their productivity higher than their peers. Among the happiness indicators examined (job satisfaction, quality of work life, life satisfaction, positive affect, and negative affect), positive affect was most strongly tied to productivity (Zelenski, et al., 2008).

Organisational level impact

Attraction and retention, performance, customer satisfaction, sickness absence, financial and reputational.

Organisational resilience

Human capital is defined in the *Social & Human Capital Protocol* as "The knowledge, skills, competencies and attributes embodied in individuals that facilitate the creation of personal, social and economic well-being" (Social & Human Capital Coalition, 2019). The quality of human capital impacts economic success. Corporate leaders and decision-makers should put people at the heart of their business strategy in order to boost their organisation's long-term resilience (Keeley, 2007). During the Covid-19 pandemic, organisations who chose to put a strong emphasis on Corporate Social Responsibility and supporting their people, positively impacted job security and as a result, organisational commitment (Filimonau et al., 2020).

Organisational performance

A study aggregated data from 339 independent research studies that include observations on the wellbeing of over a million employees and the performance of business units, from 230 independent organisations across 49 industries in 73 countries. One key finding was that employee wellbeing is consistently positively correlated with firm performance. Wellbeing had a substantial positive correlation with customer loyalty and a substantial, negative correlation with staff turnover (Krekel et al., 2019).

A happy employee is a productive employee. A study on call centre sales workers at British Telecom (BT), one of the United Kingdom's largest private employers, measured their happiness over a six-month period using a novel weekly survey instrument and linked these reports with highly detailed administrative data on workplace behaviours and various measures of employee performance. Workers made around 13% more sales in weeks where they reported being happy compared to weeks when they were unhappy. These effects are driven by workers making more calls per hour, adhering more closely to their workflow schedule, and converting more calls into sales when they are happier. (Bellet et al., 2023)

Financial returns

Return on investment research studies have estimated that there are cost savings of between $2.38 (Baxter et al., 2014) and $4 (Goetzel & Ozminkowski, 2008) for each dollar spent on wellbeing programmes. In the US Henke et al. (2011) compared data from Johnson &

Johnson with data from sixteen other large companies between 2002 and 2008. They found that Johnson & Johnson experienced a 3.7% lower average annual growth in medical costs compared to the comparison group, and that their employees had a lower average predicted probability of being at high risk for six of the nine health risks examined. Henke et al. (2011) estimated that Johnson & Johnson's EH&W programme was delivering a positive return on investment estimated at $1.88–$3.92 for every dollar spent.

Investor benefits

When employees are being cared for, they are likely to reciprocate such efforts with increased efforts (Meijman & Mulder, 1998). Goetzel et al. (2016) studied the stock market performance of companies winning the "C. Everett Koop National Health Award" – an award conferred annually to firms investing in cost-effective health and wellbeing programmes for their workers – relative to the average performance in Standard and Poor's (S&P) 500 Index. They concluded that over a period of fourteen years (2000 to 2014), winners experienced a 325% growth in stock values, whereas their equivalents experienced growth of only 105%.

Observing this strong, positive relationship between employee wellbeing, employee productivity, and firm performance it can be concluded that elevating workforce wellbeing is not in opposition to the interests of business priorities, but in fact supports their delivery. The biggest global case study where all these aspects were brought to life to demonstrate the potential impact of investing in employee health and wellbeing was the Covid-19 pandemic.

Organisational response to Covid-19 and the resulting impact on employee health and wellbeing and business success

The Covid-19 pandemic catapulted EH&W to the top of the business agenda. While the pandemic came with substantially negative consequences, including significant economic and health impact, it has also enabled the unique opportunity to lead the world's largest workplace experiment. Leaders across all industries needed to rethink and adapt how and where their employees worked, ensuring employees could do so in a safe and healthy way to ensure business continuity. How this was done and the extent to which employees felt supported, as outlined below, determined employee, managerial and organisational outcomes. This is no different from past disasters such as the Canterbury, Aotearoa, New Zealand 2010–2011 earthquakes where workplaces that supported their employees effectively had higher adaptive capacity, which facilitated organisational recovery (Nilakant et al., 2016).

Experience from past viral infections, such as seasonal influenza, taught us that there is negative impact on worker health and business productivity, through outcomes such as higher rates of sickness absence (Ip et al., 2015). How employers responded to the Covid-19 pandemic influenced employee H&W, engagement and productivity. Perceived organisational support (POS) is the magnitude to which employees believe that their organisation appraises their services and cares about their roles and the degree to which their needs are met by the organisation (Eisenberger et al., 1986). Organisational support reflects the extent to which the organisation acknowledges employees and cares about their wellbeing. It impacts individual experiences. For instance, perceived organisational support has a direct impact on nurses' occupational well-being (Zheng et al. 2024) Early on during the pandemic, a study explored views towards supportive workplace policies among employees and its association with health–related quality of life in Hong Kong. It was found that 16% reported that no workplace measures nor guidelines existed in their company related to the Covid-19 pandemic (Wong et al., 2022). Those who reported having workplace policy in place were unsatisfied with the arrangement in term of comprehensiveness (36%), timeliness (38%), and transparency (63%). These factors resulted in an increase in overall self-reported stress levels. Workplace policy and measures had a direct effect on stress, as did the perception of infection risk, which partly mediated the relationship between workplace policy and measures and health outcomes. This study highlights that protecting employee health, through robust workplace policy and measures, were important means to minimise workplace infection risk, to reduce significant stress and adverse health outcomes caused by the Covid-19 pandemic.

The extent to which an organisation protected the safety and health of its employees impacted not only health outcomes but also performance. One study of Japanese employees found that the availability of security and safety equipment were strongly and positively related to workers' wellbeing and performance and the amount of prevention measures was negatively associated with the psychological distress of the employees and positively associated with their performance, suggesting that rigorous prevention measures reduced psychological distress, protecting work outcomes (Sasaki et al., 2020).

Attracting and retaining talent

A tight labour market is one in which demand for labour is at least as strong as supply. It is a labour market in which employers compete for workers, resulting in a situation in which employee bargaining power in terms of wages and employment conditions is strong. as workers are hard to find, and the retention of current employees needs to be a high priority. The British Chambers of Commerce, in its Quarterly Recruitment Outlook survey for Q2 2021, with responses drawn from over 5700 firms, found a significant rise in those having difficulty in finding staff. While 38% of businesses surveyed said they expected to grow their workforce in the next three months, 70% of those attempting to recruit faced recruitment difficulties, rising sharply for the second consecutive quarter from 63% in Q1, which was itself a steep rise from 53% in Q4 2020. The sectors experiencing the most difficulties were construction, hotels & catering and production & manufacturing (British Chambers of Commerce, 2021). With increasing demand for workers, this challenge in filling roles will no doubt jeopardise growth and productivity. It is therefore paramount that a strong focus on employee wellbeing is prioritised, to ensure a competitive advantage in attracting staff.

Even prior to the pandemic, employees were putting greater emphasis on their wellbeing. In fact, workplace characteristics such as little stress at work or positive work–life balance have been shown to be equally, if not more, influential on employee wellbeing than pay (De Neve et al. 2018) today, as employees seek a better work–life balance and better personal wellbeing. Organisations must therefore provide support to employees in these areas to attract and retain the best talent.

The following example from UK policing's response to the Covid-19 pandemic demonstrates the impact of prioritising EH&W as part of an organisation's responses to a crisis, resulting in high employee confidence in their employer.

UK Policing – The Covid pressure test.

UK National Police Wellbeing Service (NPWS), Andy Rhodes, OBE QPM, former Chief Constable, Lancashire Police UK. Service Director National Police Wellbeing Service – Oscar Kilo. Dr Ian Hesketh, Wellbeing Lead, UK College of Policing. Senior Responsible Owner, National Police Wellbeing Service, UK.

The National Police Wellbeing Service (NPWS) has provided vital support to the national police Gold group, which was established to co-ordinate the response to Covid-19. A gold group, in policing parlance, provides strategic direction for incidents that are not day-to-day business. Large events, major incidents or the extraordinary are examples. Therefore, at a strategic level, we took ownership for procuring, supplying and developing sector-specific guidance for Personal Protective Equipment (PPE), with over 100 million items distributed over 18 months of the pandemic period. We established a Covid-19 hub area on the Oscar Kilo website (www.oscarkilo.org.uk), where policy, guidance and support could be quickly published. By locating ownership for the full range of workforce issues within the NPWS we were better able to push wellbeing to the forefront of strategic decision-making, by promoting staff engagement at every opportunity. In a sense our utility was particularly critical, mainly because of our networks and relationships developed globally over a number of years previously. In a nutshell, under pressure and with massive uncertainty, our people trusted the brand.

More than ever, organisations now realise that they have a crucial role to play in protecting people's health and enhancing their wellbeing, and are acknowledging the impact this has on business success. It is critical that employees feel cared for and supported. Organisations must therefore step up and play their part in prioritising employee health and wellbeing, in order to ensure business growth and success.

ACTIONS

1. Ensure EH&W is a core component of your people agenda, with sufficient investment to make a significant and sustainable difference.
2. All strategic business decisions that are likely to impact your people need to proactively consider and address EH&W needs.

3. Source the right EH&W expertise to address your specific business needs.
4. Ensure a comprehensive health and wellbeing approach that meets the wellbeing needs of your population.
5. Ensure that mental health is given equal parity to physical health and address the root causes of work related stress.
6. Communicate how your organisation supports EH&W internally and externally.

REFERENCES

Allen, D., Hines, E.W., Pazdernik, V., Konecny, L.T., & Breitenbach, E. (2018). Four-year review of presenteeism data among employees of a large United States health care system: A retrospective prevalence study. *Human Resources for Health*, *16*, 1–10.

Bakker, A.B. (2014). Daily fluctuations in work engagement: An overview and current directions. *European Psychologist*, *19*(4), 227–236.

Bakker, A.B., & Demerouti, E. (2008). Towards a model of work engagement. *Career Development International*, *13*(3), 209–223.

Bakker, A.B., Hakanen, J.J., Demerouti, E., & Xanthopoulou, D. (2007). Job resources boost work engagement, particularly when job demands are high. *Journal of Educational Psychology*, *99*(2), 274.

Baxter, S., Sanderson, K., Venn, A.J., Blizzard, C.L., & Palmer, A.J. (2014). The relationship between return on investment and quality of study methodology in workplace health promotion programs. *American Journal of Health Promotion*, *28*(6), 347–363.

Bellet, C.S., De Neve, J.E., & Ward, G. (2023). Does employee happiness have an impact on productivity?. *Management Science*, *70*(3), 1656–1679.

Boles, M., Pelletier, B., & Lynch, W. (2004). The relationship between health risks and work productivity. *Journal of Occupational and Environmental Medicine*, *46*(7), 737–745.

British Chambers of Commerce. (2021). Quarterly Recruitment Outlook survey for Q2 2021. Retrieved November 18, 2023 from https://www.british chambers.org.uk/news/2021/07/quarterly-recruitment-outlook-70-face-difficulty-finding-staff-as-workforce-growth-expectations-surge.

Cartwright, S., & Cooper, C.L. (Eds.). (2008). *Oxford handbook on organisational well-being*. Oxford University Press.

Chalofsky, N. E. (2010). *Meaningful workplaces: Reframing how and where we work*. New York: John Wiley & Sons.

CIPD. (2022). Health and well-being at work report 2022. Retrieved November 18, 2023 from https://www.cipd.org/globalassets/media/comms/news/ahealth-wellbeing-work-report-2022_tcm18-108440.pdf

Cooper, C., & Dewe, P. (2008). Well-being: Absenteeism, presenteeism, costs and challenges. *Occupational Medicine*, *58*(8), 522–524.

Costa, P., Passos, A. M., & Bakker, A. B. (2014). Team work engagement: A model of emergence. *Journal of Occupational and Organizational Psychology*, *87*, 414–436.

Costa, P.L., Passos, A., & Bakker, A.B. (2015). Direct and contextual influence of team conflict on team resources, team work engagement, and team performance. *Negotiation and Conflict Management Research*, *8*(4), 211–227.

De Neve, J.E., Krekel, C., & Ward, G. (2018). Work and well-being: A global perspective. *Global Happiness Policy Report*, 74–128.

Eisenberger, R., Huntington, R., Hutchison, S., & Sowa, D. (1986). Perceived organizational support. *Journal of Applied Psychology*, *71*, 500–507.

Filimonau, V., Derqui, B., & Matute, J. (2020). The COVID-19 pandemic and organisational commitment of senior hotel managers. *International Journal of Hospitality Management*, *91*, 102659.

Fredrickson, B.L. (2001). The role of positive emotions in positive psychology: The broaden-and-build theory of positive emotions. *American Psychologist*, *56*, 218–226.

Fredrickson, B.L., & Joiner, T. (2002). Positive emotions trigger upward spirals toward emotional well-being. *Psychological Science*, *13*, 172–175.

Gallup. (2023). State of the global workplace: 2023 report. Retrieved January 19, 2024 from https://www.gallup.com/workplace/349484/state–of–the-global-workplace.aspx

Gawke, J.C.L., Gorgievski, M.J., & Bakker, A.B. (2017). Employee intrapreneurship and work engagement: A latent change score approach. *Journal of Vocational Behavior*, *100*, 88–100.

Goetzel, R.Z., Fabius, R., Fabius, D., Roemer, E.C., Thornton, N., Kelly, R.K., & Pelletier, K.R. (2016). The stock performance of C. Everett Koop award winners compared with the Standard & Poor's 500 index. *Journal of Occupational and Environmental Medicine*, *58*(1), 9–15.

Goetzel, R.Z., Long, S.R., Ozminkowski, R.J., Hawkins, K., Wang, S., & Lynch, W. (2004). Health, absence, disability, and presenteeism cost estimates of certain physical and mental health conditions affecting U.S. employers. *Journal of Occupational and Environmental Medicine*, *46*(4), 398–412.

Goetzel, R.Z., & Ozminkowski, R.J. (2008). Health, absence, disability, and presenteeism cost estimates of certain physical and mental health conditions affecting U.S. employers. *Journal of Occupational and Environmental Medicine*, *46*(4), 398–412.

Goh, J., Pfeffer, J., Zenios, S.A., & Rajpal, S. (2015). Workplace stressors & health outcomes: Health policy for the workplace. *Behavioral Science & Policy*, *1*(1), 43–52.

Halbesleben, J.R.B., & Wheeler, A.R. (2008). The relative roles of engagement and embeddedness in predicting job performance and intention to leave. *Work & Stress*, *22*, 242–256.

Health and Safety at Work etc. Act 1974, Pub. L. No. 37, § 2. Retrieved November 18, 2023, from https://www.legislation.gov.uk/ukpga/1974/37/section/2

Health and Safety Executive. (n.d.). *Standards for work-related stress*. Health and Safety Executive. Retrieved November 18, 2023, from https://www.hse.gov.uk/stress/standards/index.htm

Henke, R.M., Goetzel, R.Z., McHugh, J., & Isaac, F. (2011). Recent experience in health promotion at Johnson & Johnson: Lower health spending, strong return on investment. *Health Affairs, 30*(3), 490–499.

Ip, D.K., Lau, E.H., Tam, Y.H., So, H.C., Cowling, B.J., & Kwok, H.K. (2015). Increases in absenteeism among health care workers in Hong Kong during influenza epidemics, 2004–2009. *BMC Infectious Diseases, 15,* 1–9.

Isen, A.M., & Baron, R.A. (1991). Positive affect as a factor in organizational behavior. In Staw, B.M., & Cummings, L.L. (Eds.), *Research in organizational behavior.* Greenwich, CT: JAI Press.

Jackson, T. (2019). The post-growth challenge: Secular stagnation, inequality and the limits to growth. *Ecological Economics, 156,* 236–246.

Kahn, W.A. (1990). Psychological conditions of personal engagement and disengagement at work. *Academy of Management Journal, 33*(4), 692–724.

Keeley, B. (2007). Human capital: How what you know shapes your life. In *OECD insights.* Paris: OECD Publishing.

Krekel, C., Ward, G., de Neve, J.-E., Harter, J., Blankson, A., Clark, A., Cooper, C., Lim, J., Litchfield, P., Moss, J., Norton, M., Whillans, A., Cooperrider, D., & Mendlewicz, D. (2019). Employee wellbeing, productivity, and firm performance. In *Global happiness and wellbeing policy report.* New York: Sustainable Development Solutions Network, 72–94.

Maslach, C., & Leiter, M.P. (1997). *The Truth about burnout: How organizations cause personal stress and what to do about it.* San Francisco, CA: Jossey-Bass.

Meijman, T.F., & Mulder, G. (1998). Psychological aspects of workload. In P.J.D. Drenth, H. Thierry, & C.J. De Wolff (Eds.), *The handbook of work and organizational psychology: Work psychology*(pp. 5–33). London, UK: Psychology Press.

Nilakant, V., Walker, B., Kuntz, J., de Vries, H.P., Malinen, S., Näswall, K., & van Heugten, K. (2016). Dynamics of organizational response to a disaster: A study of organizations impacted by earthquakes. In C.M. Hall, S. Malinen, & R. Wordsworth (Eds.), *Business and postdisaster management* (pp. 35–47). London, UK: Routledge.

Norris-Green, M., & Gifford, J. (2021). *CIPD good work index 2021.* London: Chartered Institute of Personnel and Development.

Rich, B.L., LePine, J.A., & Crawford, E.R. (2010). Job engagement: Antecedents and effects on job performance. *Academy of Management Journal, 53,* 617–635.

Richardsen, A.M., Burke, R.J., & Martinussen, M. (2006). Work and health outcomes among police officers: The mediating role of police cynicism and engagement. *International Journal of Stress Management, 13*(4), 555–574.

Robertson, I.T., & Cooper, C.L. (2010). Full engagement: The integration of employee engagement and psychological well-being. *Leadership & Organization Development Journal, 31*(4), 324–336.

Robinson, D., Perryman, S., & Hayday, S. (2004). *The drivers of employee engagement.* Report 408. UK: Institute for Employment Studies.

Rothbard, N., & Wilk, S. (2011). Waking up on the right or wrong side of the bed: Start-of-workday mood, work events, employee affect, and performance. *The Academy of Management Journal, 54*(5), 959–980.

Ryan, R.M., & Deci, E.L. (2000). Self-determination theory and the facilitation of intrinsic motivation, social development, and well-being. *American Psychologist, 55,* 68–78.

Ryff, C.D., & Keyes, C.L.M. (1995). The structure of psychological well-being revisited. *Journal of Personality and Social Psychology, 69*(4), 719–727.

Sasaki, N., Kuroda, R., Tsuno, K., & Kawakami, N. (2020). Workplace responses to COVID-19 associated with mental health and work performance of employees in Japan. *Journal of Occupational Health, 62*(1), e12134.

Schaufeli, W.R., & Bakker, A.B. (2004). Job demands and job resources and their relationship with burnout and engagement: A multiple-sample study.

Seligman, M.E.P. (2011). *Flourish: A visionary new understanding of happiness and well-being.* New York, NY: Free Press.

Shuck, B., & Reio, T.G. (2014). Employee engagement and well-being: A moderation model and implications for practice. *Journal of Leadership & Organizational Studies, 21*(1), 43–58.

Social & Human Capital Coalition. (2019). *Social & human capital protocol.* Retrieved November 18, 2023, from https://capitalscoalition.org/capitals-approach/social-human-capital-protocol/

Sonnentag, S. (2015). Dynamics of well-being. *Annual Review of Organizational Psychology and Organizational Behavior, 2*(1), 261–293.

Staw, B.M., & Barsade, S.G. (1993). Affect and managerial performance: A test of the sadder-but-wiser vs. happier-and-smarter hypotheses. *Administrative Science Quarterly, 38,* 304–331.

Street, L., Uddin, A., Wallace, M., Lee, M., & Angle, A. (2021). *Everyone benefits: Connecting health and safety and human capital.* The SustainAbility Institute by ERM. Retrieved November 18, 2023, from: https://www.erm.com/globalassets/sustainability.com/thinking/pdfs/ermsi-healthandsafety-report.pdf

Turban, D.B., & Yan, W. (2016). Relationship of eudaimonia and hedonia with work outcomes. *Journal of Managerial Psychology, 31*(6), 1006–1020.

Wong, E.L.Y., Ho, K.F., Wong, S.Y.S., Cheung, A.W.L., Yau, P.S.Y., Dong, D., & Yeoh, E.K. (2022). Views on workplace policies and its impact on health-related quality of life during coronavirus disease (COVID-19) pandemic: Cross-sectional survey of employees. *International Journal of Health Policy and Management, 11*(3), 344–353.

Wright, T.A., & Cropanzano, R. (2000). Psychological well-being and job satisfaction as predictors of job performance. *Journal of Occupational Health Psychology, 5*(1), 84–94

Xanthopoulou, D., Bakker, A.B., Demerouti, E., & Schaufeli, W.B. (2009). Work engagement and financial returns: A diary study on the role of job and personal resources. *Journal of Occupational and Organizational Psychology, 82*(1), 183–200.

Young, J. (2023). *CIPD good work index 2023: Summary report.* London: Chartered Institute of Personnel and Development.

Zelenski, J.M., Murphy, S.A., & Jenkins, D.A. (2008). The happy-productive worker thesis revisited. *Journal of Happiness Studies, 9*, 521–537.

Zheng, J., Feng, S., Gao, R. et al. (2024). The relationship between organizational support, professional quality of life, decent work, and professional well-being among nurses: A cross-sectional study. *BMC Nursing 23*, 425.

2

EMPLOYEE HEALTH AND WELLBEING MUST BE A TOP COMPANY PRIORITY

Key messages

1. Prioritising employee health and wellbeing starts with integrating a comprehensive and proactive approach into business strategies.
2. The CEO has a fundamental role in positioning employee health and wellbeing as a top company priority and setting expectations that everyone, at every level of the organisation, including the executive team must play their part in supporting this agenda.
3. The executive team, must act as a catalyst, driving the employee health and wellbeing agenda through their respective organisations and reviewing business-level EH&W metrics regularly to inform the approach.
4. A passionate executive sponsor of employee health and wellbeing can champion, advocate for and keep employee health and wellbeing on the executive, and therefore business, agenda.
5. Embedding a positive health and wellbeing culture requires activation of the entire ecosystem, engaging all stakeholders with an interest in and influence on the EH&W agenda. As a result, the health and wellbeing of employees becomes part of the DNA of the organisation, business as usual and a key consideration when making business decisions.

DOI: 10.4324/9781003124979-2

INTRODUCTION

Despite the health and wellbeing of employees having risen to top of the organisational agenda during the Covid-19 pandemic, resulting in greater awareness, and in some cases investment, there is much more to be done. The UK CIPD's Health and Wellbeing at Work report 2021 gathered insights from 668 HR professionals spanning the private (55%), public (28%) and voluntary (17%) sectors. The report encouragingly found that as a result of the pandemic there has been a step change in the proportion of senior leaders that have employee wellbeing on their agenda (75%, up from 61% in 2020) and additionally a fall in the proportion that report their organisation is 'much more reactive than proactive'. While public sector organisations seem to be most proactive on wellbeing, nearly half (46%) of organisations surveyed still lacked a formal strategy or approach to health and wellbeing and acted on an ad hoc basis (CIPD, 2021). All organisations should reflect upon, review and revise existing commitment levels in order to take a longer-term, strategic approach. So what does commitment to wellbeing actually mean?

CREATING A CULTURE OF WELLBEING: THE EIGHT FACTORS

1. *Embed employee health and wellbeing into the business agenda*

Commitment from the top of the house influences the extent to which health and wellbeing is driven through the organisation. Best practices include embedding wellbeing into the business agenda, supported by a clear strategy, goals and plans on how they will be achieved. Three case studies from public and private sector organisations exemplify significant commitment to the health and wellbeing agenda:

British Petroleum

"Improving people's lives" – Integrating Wellbeing in BP's Transformation Journey.

Dr Richard Heron – Independent Medical Advisor and former Chief Medical Officer, British Petroleum

Bp is a multinational energy company with over 63,000 employees in 72 countries that delivers heat, light and mobility products and services to customers around the world.

In February 2020, just before the WHO declared Covid-19 a public health emergency of international concern, bp launched its new purpose to "reimagine energy for people and planet", with an ambitious net zero ambition and aims. Aligned with this new direction, plans were introduced to see bp fundamentally transform from an International Oil Company to an Integrated Energy Company, embarking on possibly the most significant strategic change in its history.

Entering a global pandemic right at the beginning of this journey was undoubtedly a significant challenge, but also presented "once in a generation" opportunities to make health and wellbeing central to business success.

How have health and wellbeing plans been integrated into the business agenda? Embedded in bp's transformation journey and published in bp's 2020 sustainability report are 20 aims that we have set. The first ten focus on getting bp to net zero carbon emissions by 2050 or sooner and helping the world get there too. Alongside these are five to care for our planet and five aims to help improve people's lives.

In this group, Aim 15 is to *enhance the health and wellbeing of our employees, contractors and local communities.* The thinking behind each aim was informed by the United Nations Sustainable Development Goals (SDGs): in the case of Aim 15, SDG 3 (Good health and wellbeing), SDG 8 (Decent work and economic growth), SDG 10 (Reduced inequalities) and SDG 17 (Partnership for the goals). The Goals helped us to focus our efforts where the most meaningful contribution could be made over the next ten years. Drawing on bp's health and wellbeing team's capabilities in public health, occupational health and industrial hygiene, physical and mental wellbeing objectives, targets and plans through to 2025 were developed, as well as aspirations for 2030.

The three wellbeing objectives are to:

1. Promote proactive measures to improve the health and wellbeing of our workforce and their families.
2. Improve awareness and understanding of mental health challenges in the workplace and broader community.
3. Create access to and build awareness of physical and mental health resources in the communities where we work.

Taking care of mental health and wellbeing can be seen as a fundamental consideration in bp's journey of transformation.

All organisational transformations bring with them change, uncertainty and reduced control for employees. In February 2020, however, few could have predicted the extent to which the Covid-19 pandemic would make uncertainty about the future a shared feeling for everyone on the planet. The importance of helping everybody with these and other challenges to mental and physical health have been at the heart of bp's organisational responses to the pandemic.

Examples of actions taken in the last year in service of these objectives include:

- increasing the use of opportunities to keep connected in a "locked-down" world.
- availability, scope and, with them, the utilisation of global employee assistance programmes were increased to support people.
- a global physical activity challenge helped teams stay connected and active during global, pandemic "lockdowns" – almost 6000 people from about 60 countries competed together, virtually and in teams.

Specific guidance provided to bp people ranged from information about the symptoms of Covid-19 to the provision of home working resources. Guides and podcasts also helped people manage their own physical and mental health challenges.

With many working still working from sites in critical infrastructure roles throughout the pandemic, it was especially important to provide them specific support, particularly those who were isolated in remote locations.

Since 2020 over 18,500 employees across bp have attended training sessions to improve some aspect of their awareness, understanding and skills in managing mental health.

The approach to improving people's lives at bp is and remains people-centred, data-led and underpinned by specific targets. For example, commitments are in place to train all leaders on key mental health challenges to foster a culture of care; the ultimate aim is to demonstrate a positive shift in awareness and understanding of mental health challenges as a result of our programmes.

"Care" has also been integrated in other key strategic areas such as bp's safety leadership principles; "together, we genuinely care about each other" is one such principle – and, delving a little deeper, this is defined as:

- We care about everybody's safety as if they are our own family.
- We show care by looking out for each other.
- We help others to see unsafe situations when they may not.

Actions to raise awareness of mental health and make it easier to access support have contributed to reducing stigma. In addition to signing up to national (in the UK MIND's "Time to change") and global (the Global Business Collaboration's CEO) pledges, bp's executive leadership and a diverse spectrum of our global workforce have actively shared personal, "lived" experiences, all of which have made it easier for our people to speak up and get help when struggling.

While we have made great progress, there is of course much more to do in support of better health and wellbeing for the benefit of employees, their families, and the success of the company and the wider economy.

UK policing

UK Policing: Mandating Health and Wellbeing Throughout the Organisation.

Dr Ian Hesketh and Constable Andy Rhodes – National Police Wellbeing Service

We have now integrated our health and wellbeing priorities into the first ever Police Covenant to be enshrined in law. This leverages support, as does the inclusion of health and wellbeing into the police force inspection regime. It should be noted that we lineate in that we lead horses to water and help them drink, but we do not inspect. We maintain our position on this to avoid health and wellbeing in the National Police Wellbeing Service (NPWS) being seen as coercive, though in some camps this may seem inevitable as the value of good strategy becomes ever more vivid.

The NPWS Programme is intrinsically linked to, and mutually supportive of, the forthcoming Police Covenant. The six live services deliver capability that meets the Police Covenant's objective to deliver improved "Wellbeing & Health" (Theme 2) to police officers and staff. The programme is also leading on the production of best practice guidelines for "Support for Families" (Theme 3).

NHS

Wrightington, Wigan and Leigh Teaching Hospitals NHS Foundation Trust.

Zoe Garnett – Staff Wellbeing Manager

Towards the end of 2021, WWL signed up to the newly launched NHS Wellbeing Pledges. The work required to implement these pledges so far has included:

- Embedding person-centred, holistic wellbeing into organisational policy frameworks to facilitate whole organisational culture change. WWL has introduced a specific Wellbeing pillar as part of our Trust Strategy leading up to 2030 and a Strategic Wellbeing Working Group linking into this to ensure the work is embedded throughout the Trust.
- Leadership development designed to support our leaders in this approach.

2. *Leverage CEO influence*

A CEO who appreciates the value of prioritising EH&W can influence the EH&W agenda in multiple ways, such as being a visible champion, role modelling positive behaviours, storytelling, setting expectations of the executive team to drive the EH&W agenda forward and of all employees to play a role in enhancing their own health and wellbeing.

Through means such as these, CEOs can create a culture of positive wellbeing across the organisation. The following case study showcases the potential the power of a Chief Executive in activating the entire organisation, with resulting impacts across the organisation.

Gloucestershire NHS Trust: The impact of CEO leadership in health and wellbeing: Deborah's story.

Deborah Lee. Chief Executive, Gloucestershire NHS Trust

Gloucestershire NHS Trust in the UK has approximately 9000 employees and serves 630,000 members of the public.

Deborah Lee, Chief Executive of Gloucestershire NHS Trust, decided to open up in 2018 about the period of mental illness that she had experienced ten years earlier. She did this through her Chief Exec internal blog, in which she described her acute illness that led her to experience anxiety, impacted on her work and required her to take sickness absence from work and access professional support. With the support of her manager, she was able to make a successful and rapid return to work. She did recall, however, that her manager suggested that she keep the reason for her absence to herself due to concerns about perceptions.

Her decision for wanting to come out about her illness was during a lightbulb moment when she became the Chief Executive and reflected upon the leadership qualities and purpose of her role. She came to the conclusion that she did not want to hide that side of herself. Wanting to set the tone of the trust, she realised that cultural change starts at the top.

Her aim was to help end the stigma, to help people to feel able to share their stories without negative consequences, allowing people permission to be themselves at work and seek needed support early to minimise the impact of their condition.

The response from her blog was unprecedented. She received more emails from this one blog than she had in the past two years, this led to her producing a vlog in which she talked about her experience as part of the trust's activities to promote World Mental Health Day. Feedback when she walked the shopfloor was hugely positive, resulting in many people across all levels of staff being inspired to relate their stories with her and also sharing that they, as a result, sought mental health support.

She acknowledges that there is still more work to be done in this space due to mental health being still being seen as a weakness and vulnerability by many, including those who suffer it themselves.

What Deborah continues to do to keep mental wellbeing on the agenda:

- The 'Ask twice' campaign. This is an initiative developed by a mental health charity which highlighted that people are more likely to open up after being asked a second time about how they are feeling. Deborah launched this initiative on her blog on World Mental Health Day.

She brings the 'Ask twice' campaign alive through her daily interactions with people. She opens with "How is it going for you?" The default response from an employee is often what they think she wants to hear such as "I am OK", to which she often replies through highlighting her current challenges: "It has been tough for me recently because of …" as a result of which people start to open up.

- She continues to write blogs on mental health.
- Wellbeing metrics are reviewed at board level (see below).

Through her passion, actions, and influence, the Chief Executive of Gloucestershire NHS Trust, Deborah Lee, has made significant positive cultural changes within her trust. Below we can find more examples of how she achieved this.

3. Appoint a board-level sponsor with clear responsibilities

A board-level sponsor advocates for EH&W, ensuring it remains on the agenda of the board. Choosing a sponsor that has a passion for wellbeing is paramount; otherwise it becomes an onerous and often neglected task. The National Health Service (NHS), the government-funded medical and health care service in the UK, is leading the way. The NHS employs more than 1.2 million full-time equivalent staff working in NHS trusts in England. Health Education England published a Mental Wellbeing Commissioned Report for those learning in the NHS, as well as those currently working within the NHS (Health Education England, 2019). The first recommendation was the need for board-level leadership to be responsible for the mental wellbeing of their staff. It was anticipated that this should be an existing executive director who would be aligned with a non-executive director. It was recommended in this report that each NHS Trust has a Workforce Wellbeing Guardian and follows the nine principles outlined below.

Despite being developed for NHS trusts, these principles together form a strong foundation that can be incorporated within any organisation that wants to prioritise wellbeing.

Principle One: The mental health and wellbeing of NHS staff and those learning in the NHS should not be compromised by the work they do for the NHS.

Principle Two: The Wellbeing Guardian will ensure that where there is an individual or team exposure to a clinical event that is particularly distressing, time is made available to check the wellbeing impact on those NHS staff and learners.

Principle Three: The Wellbeing Guardian will ensure that wellbeing 'check-in' meetings will be provided to all new staff on appointment and to all learners on placement in the NHS as outlined in the Commission's recommendations.

Principle Four: All NHS staff and those learning in the NHS will have ready access to a self-referral, proactive and confidential occupational health service that promotes and protects wellbeing.

Principle Five: The death by suicide of any member of staff or a learner working in an NHS organisation will be independently examined and the findings reported through the Wellbeing Guardian to the board.

Principle Six: The NHS will ensure that all staff and learners have an environment that is both safe and supportive of their mental wellbeing.

Principle Seven: The NHS will ensure that the cultural and spiritual needs of its staff and those learning in the NHS are protected and will ensure equitable and appropriate wellbeing support for overseas staff and learners who are working in the NHS.

Principle Eight: The NHS will ensure the wellbeing and make the necessary adjustments for the nine groups protected under the Equality Act 2010

Principle Nine: The Wellbeing Guardian, working with system leaders and regulators, will ensure that wellbeing is given equal weight in organisational performance assessment.

Gloucestershire NHS Trust.

Chief Executive – Deborah Lee

It matters to people working in Gloucestershire NHS Trust that their Chief Executive and leaders care. The Trust, as per the requirement of all NHS trusts, now has a 'Wellbeing Guardian' at board level to support the CEO to drive the agenda forward.

All organisations need to strongly consider appointing an executive sponsor for EH&W.

4. Appoint a health and wellbeing board

The role of a health and wellbeing board is to develop an EH&W strategy including plans on how to execute this, and to gain board-level sponsorship and commitment to help deliver of the strategy. This involves identifying existing and emerging trends in employee health and wellbeing that could enhance or pose a risk to business success, and proactively developing solutions. Identifying focus areas, setting targets and reviewing progress are common activities conducted through this board. The two cases below bring this to life:

SE Coast Ambulance NHS Trust: Establishing a Health and Wellbeing Board.

Angela Raynor – former Head of H&W SE coast NHS Trust

A trust-wide Health and Wellbeing Programme Board was established in October 2021 with a focus on embedding health and wellbeing strategies and considerations into trust decision-making, policies, procedures and processes reducing stigma around ill-health, and recognising and seeking to minimise the on-the-job realities that impact on us on a day-to-day basis. This will contribute to the prevention agenda. The board is responsible for monitoring the progress of the health and wellbeing agenda and making key strategic decisions that impact employee health and wellbeing.

Membership includes the trust-appointed executive Wellbeing Guardian (non-executive director) and union representation.

Gloucestershire NHS Trust's People Committee.

Deborah Lee – Chief Executive

Following observations that 'people' conversations were happening as an 'add on' at other committees a separate board 'People Committee' was set up two years ago to provide assurance to the board that the people agenda was prioritised, and progress reviewed.

One example of a board decision to enhance staff wellbeing was around support for subsidised food. There was national funding for subsidised food, and NHS staff reported that they appreciated the opportunity to take a physical break from their ward or department and have some downtime in the staff restaurant. When national funding ended the People Committee successfully advocated for reprioritising the trust budget and re-instigated the 50% subsidy on food.

5. Engage the executive team to deliver the EH&W agenda

The role of the executive team is to advocate for, sponsor and support delivery of the EH&W strategy across their respective businesses. Workplace wellness programmes can deliver benefits in terms of enhanced productivity, but this is reliant on certain conditions being met, including senior management support (Isham et al., 2020). Senior managers must show support, through involvement and commitment to EH&W initiatives, role model positive behaviours and set expectations that employees nurture their wellbeing and support them to do so. As these filter down the organisation, it will undoubtedly have an impact, such as positive cultural change, improved employee engagement, satisfaction, retention and net promoter score and enhanced employee – manager relationships.

Ways in which the executive team can create a positive employee health and wellbeing culture:

a) Connecting with staff on the shopfloor

Wrightington Wigan and Leigh Teaching Hospitals NHS Foundation Trust.

Zoe Garnett – Staff Wellbeing Manager

Executive wellbeing walks – On a fortnightly basis, one of our Executive Team is joined by a Wellbeing Lead to facilitate a wellbeing walkabout. These happen across our hospital and community sites throughout the year with a different site being visited at each walkabout. The walkabouts have a few purposes, including:

- for our senior leaders to be a listening ear and really hear what staff have to say when they are asked "How are you?"
- to share good wellbeing practice that is happening across the Trust
- for feedback to be given to our Steps4Wellness team as to what further support is needed at site/department/team level and for targeted support to be arranged
- to embed wellbeing into our everyday conversations and organisational culture

The walkabouts are valued by our staff and leaders alike and have really made a difference to the morale and engagement of those staff already visited.

b) Request and Review wellbeing metrics

While many organisations make significant investments in EH&W, few actually measure their impact (Goetzel & Ozminkowski, 2008) which could go some way to explaining the neutrality or even scepticism regarding the value of investment in EH&W. Organisations that engage in some form of measurement usually limit their focus to usage and satisfaction measures, missing the opportunity to demonstrate individual and organisational value. This could however would position EH&W as a strategic enabler of sustainable high performance and therefore business success (McGillivray, 2002).

Reviewing data, both qualitative and quantitative, ensures resources are utilised most effectively. Data should be sought to identify EH&W needs, target populations most at risk and track impact. The following three examples highlight how data can provide key insights to guide actions, accountability and impact.

Using data to target those that need support the most:

- **At Gloucestershire NHS Trust** the board's People Committee has been a conduit for reviewing staff wellbeing, using a dashboard for people metrics that include turnover, sickness absence rates and reasons, use of the counselling service, 20:20 Hub data and staff surveys. The trust is currently piloting a "cultural barometer" which involves doing a temperature check of teams, wards or departments. Employees are asked five questions that align to the national staff survey on areas such as engagement, manager support, bullying and wellbeing. The aim is to identify "hot zones", following which psychologists and organisational development practitioners can provide support to a ward or department to observe, offering face-to-face consultations or team briefings for instance.

Using data to demonstrate impact:

- **Serco Group plc** specialises in the delivery of essential public services, with over 50,000 people working in defence, transport, justice, immigration, healthcare and other citizen services across four regions: UK & Europe, North America, Asia Pacific and the Middle East.

Serco Group PLC's Wellbeing Manager Finau Vucago and Kym Bancroft, Serco's Head of Health, Safety, Environment and Wellbeing:

"We find it easiest to land wellbeing from the place with the strongest gravitational pull for the organisation. At Serco exec level this is through the Health & Safety frame. Given the nature of the business H&S is a key priority and Senior Leaders are well versed in our language and narrative around safety. Presenting wellbeing initiatives with similar language & narrative enables understanding & thus deeper analysis of the challenges and solutions. We report our wellbeing dashboard to the Executive Committee and our wellbeing risks & controls to the Corporate Risk Committee quarterly to ensure they are always in the conversation." Measures reported include the percentage of managers that have completed their training, company survey indicators of trust and psychological safety, sickness absence, health-related claims and counselling service usage.

Using data to track progress and drive accountability and ownership:

- **UK Policing: Dr Ian Hesketh and Constable Andy Rhodes – National Police Wellbeing Service:**

"The availability of meaningful data which accurately tracks progress remains an ongoing challenge, and our focus has been to establish the national survey, detailed above, as our primary source of data to help us prioritise finite funding and resources. At individual force level (there are 43 forces in England & Wales) there are good examples of data being taken down to a more granular level. This allows senior leaders to adopt a more thoughtful and reflective style of enquiry, as opposed to a binary performance management response. Following the national survey results we engage with numerous forces to effectively deep dive into their own results, identifying trends and comparing with the national picture.

For example, in Lancashire Police the data collected from workforce surveying over six years makes the link between key drivers of engagement and wellbeing whilst providing analysis by gender, ethnicity, role, geo-location and age. Visual presentation is very important and must seek to replicate the way all other business information is utilised if we are to expect our managers to navigate it usefully. High-impact mapping of wellbeing and engagement data creates a sense of 'this is real' which in turn drives ownership and accountability to address that which is within the control of the local leadership team. These insights have been proven to inform interventions which have, in turn, improved key areas year on year.

Survey data is a means to an end, not simply an end in itself and so the action taken must be visible to the workforce, so that trust in the processes around employee voice builds over time. The surveys also provide a rich source of leadership training material, with our first line, middle managers and executives able to see the results of the working environmental conditions for themselves, in their own back yards so to speak. This also provides an excellent learning resource, so they can fully understand the impact of good work on wellbeing, and of course wellbeing on good work.

The underpinning notion is that line managers have a huge influence on health and wellbeing and we probe 'feeling valued' at different levels of leadership in our surveys."

c) Engage with employee representatives

Executive team member presence at employee representative meetings will allow employees to feel heard in relation to work issues that impact them, and provide support. The example below is from SUEZ recycling and recovery UK:

SUEZ recycling and recovery UK.

Dr Tracey Leghorn – Chief Business Services Officer and Natalie Sáenz – SW Regional Communications Manager

SUEZ recycling and recovery UK employs over 6,000 people and handles approximately 10 million tonnes of waste materials every year. Through collection, treatment, recycling and logistics operations, it serves more than 30,000 business customers and millions of householders throughout the country.

Operating in over 300 locations – from household waste recycling centres and transfer stations to energy-from-waste, recycling, re-use, composting and secure shredding facilities – SUEZ provides an extensive range of services covering the whole process of waste management, from initial consultancy through to collection and treatment. The majority of its employees are on the frontline, predominantly male – emptying bins, driving, or working in facilities with factory-like settings.

The SUEZ Works Council is a committee composed of elected employee representatives from SUEZ recycling and recovery UK and with members of the Management Board as employer members. Employee representatives represent the views and opinions of employees within their constituency and feedback issues raised by employees to the management. There are 19 employee representatives within 13 constituencies across the UK, including Scotland, Northern Ireland and the Isle of Man.

The purpose to the SUEZ recycling and recovery UK Works Council is to inform and consult employee representatives at all levels in the UK and the Isle of Man on issues that will, or are likely to, affect the company's employees in the future. It provides a forum that enables employees, through their employee representatives, to contribute to the continuous improvement of SUEZ recycling and recovery UK and our working environment.

6. Invest in EH&W expertise to set and deliver a comprehensive EH&W strategy

Driving the EHW agenda, developing a comprehensive strategy and deciding which services to offer requires expertise to ensure that the focus is on the right issues, which when addressed, will significantly enhance EHW&W, engagement and productivity. Experts will additionally look for the most impactful solutions and measure the effectiveness of these. The following example shows how a coordinated approach using expertise, had positive workforce impact, that is consistent, even in the most complex of organisations.

UK Policing: Starting the Cultural Change Journey.

Andy Rhodes – OBE QPM, Chief Constable of Lancashire Constabulary and National Police Lead on Wellbeing, and Dr. Ian Hesketh – Wellbeing Lead, UK College of Policing

The National Police Wellbeing Service (NPWS) was conceived, developed, and launched by the [then] Chief Constable of Lancashire Constabulary and National Police lead on Wellbeing, Andy Rhodes QPM and Dr. Ian Hesketh, a former police officer and academic. The concept was to create a vehicle by which to take this previously unexplored (in UK policing) phenomena of wellbeing forward and to develop it into being viewed in policing as business as usual. Following extensive research, pilot work and funding applications, the service, known as *Oscar Kilo*, was officially launched in 2019.

Initially, the service was funded via a police transformation fund grant from the UK Home Office. This is a standard approach in policing for new initiatives that are to become mainstream once proof of concept and efficacy are established. Therefore, an extensive programme board and associated project management resources were established to support this journey to mainstream.

At its heart, the NPWS consists of a series of coordinated activities, planned events and related measures that provide evidence of operational effectiveness. These aspects all focus on the aim to deliver the *Common Goal for Police Wellbeing* vision, associated change, and benefits of a holistic approach to psychological health and wellbeing. The objective is to support police forces to sustainably grow and manage their workforce.

By recognising there are structural challenges to delivering change across a workforce of approximately 200,000 people (and this number is growing under an *Uplift* programme to introduce 20,000 more police officers), who are situated within 43 independently controlled police forces, the preference was to adopt a '*systems leadership*' approach. It has been critically important to work smartly within the confines of a complex, hierarchical environment whilst also building powerful networks of influence both internally and externally.

The internal networks are comprised of staff associations, unions, charities and influential stakeholders in police forces, the Home Office and the Association of Police and Crime Commissioners. The NPWS engagement team was established to access and support these multiple channels to provide clarity on what is provided. This includes advice on what works (and what does not) and also to help innovators to gain valuable exposure and advocacy. Built around an open-source website (www.oscarkilo.org.uk), the accessibility and visibility of the training programmes, events, self-assessment frameworks and associated guidance documents attracts between 200 and 300 site visits per day, peaking to over 1000 people per day during the Covid-19 pandemic. Our website analytics provide us with fantastic insight into the who, where and what in terms of website traffic. These analytics are essential in our strategic management of the programme and associated live services. All the UK Police Forces can also book one of the 10 outreach vans via our website, currently undergoing a complete refresh to reflect user experiences and future utility.

7. Activate all levels of the organisation to bring the strategy to life

For maximal impact, there needs to be a holistic, company-wide, integrated approach to EH&W:

British Telecom: Bringing the strategy to life.

Dr Richard Caddis – Chief Medical Officer

Preventative campaigns are a key approach in raising the visibility and encouraging conversations around mental health at work. We have discussed the importance (also shown in evidence) of the role of the executive team and senior leaders in setting the tone, but at BT we have recognised that the amplification and embedding of a culture of wellbeing requires colleagues from all levels in the organisation to be actively involved. We developed mental health awareness training for managers, which continued to be delivered during the pandemic as well as the launch of wellbeing champions across all areas of the business. These champions had training on the strategy and programme from the health, safety and wellbeing centre of expertise as well as a deeper understanding of support services. This allows them to not only support campaigns at a local level but embed the signposting for operational managers. Our professional network of peer support is also a valued resource to managers, with over 300 trained peers across the business, who benefit from a professional clinical oversight and programme of development. We recognise the role management plays in this is critical. Our vision is to develop confidence, competence and ability to recognise and signpost. This has launched with awareness training, focus on the impact of mindfulness on mental health, and the importance of connectedness. Specific tailored topics to support specific cultural needs and specific mental health topics have engaged our leaders in recognising the benefits of the approach – bringing the strategy to life.

In this example from British Telecom, cultural change required activating of all levels of the organisation.

Holistic Approach
Implementing health and wellbeing solutions

Figure 2.1 The holistic approach to wellbeing

A comprehensive approach to EH&W requires involvement from all levels. Examples include: at the Organisational level; developing EH&W policies, company-wide wellbeing communications such as blogs by executives, campaigns and sharing company wellbeing commitments; Line Manager level; training, coaching, peer networks; at the Team level; agreement on EH&W objectives undertaking a team stress risk assessment and identifying actions to mitigate risks, undertaking a self-care or healthy behaviours course together; and at the Individual level, discussing wellbeing commitments with their line manager and colleagues, attending a wellbeing course, using the available counselling service or speaking to the company occupational health expert for health-related advice.

8. Take an ecosystem approach to employee wellbeing

Everybody is accountable for positive wellbeing in the workplace. Often, within an organisation, different functions play a role in enhancing EH&W, often in a siloed fashion. This can result in a fragmented approach, where the very employees, who these groups are targeting, receive multiple unconnected EH&W communications and messaging. Bringing these groups together around a common vision and strategy, will ensure an aligned, consistent and more impactful approach, that enhances employee awareness and uptake of EH&W offerings available.

Highlighting key groups that have a stake in employee health wellbeing, connecting them and clarifying their roles and responsibilities will avoid duplication and enable an integrated and holistic approach. Identify all key groups and functions that influence workforce health and wellbeing and coordinate efforts.

Figure 2.2 The wellbeing stakeholder ecosystem

The table below highlights some of the ways in which key stakeholders can drive the employee health and wellbeing (EH&W) agenda forward:

Stakeholder	Enabler
Senior leadership	— Position EH&W as a company priority and integrate EH&W into the business agenda. — Identify executive sponsors for wellbeing and sponsor an EH&W committee/board. — Review EH&W metrics regularly at board level. — Invest in the right EH&W expertise to identify which evidence-based wellbeing resources to offer to employees. — Role model positive H&W practices and Personal Storytelling. — Promote the importance of wellbeing and resources available in company-wide communications. — Position EH&W is a key leadership competency and hire and promote managers based on this capability in this skill in addition to their technical skills. — Give managers time to attend training and peer group sessions and enable them to invest in their own wellbeing during the workday where practical.
Line manager	— Role model positive self-care practices. — Check-in regularly with employees to discuss their wellbeing. — Create an environment of psychological safety to enable employees to open up. — Undertake available manager training on EH&W. — Give employees time to attend training and peer group sessions and enable them to invest in their wellbeing during the workday.

(Continued)

Stakeholder	Enabler
All employees	– Discuss wellbeing needs with their manager.
	– Support colleagues with their wellbeing.
	– Engage with available wellbeing resources and training opportunities.
	– Share effective wellbeing strategies with others.
	– Join/create relevant wellbeing networks to bring people together, such as Employee Resource Groups.
HR	– Be a sponsor of and promote wellbeing to leaders and employees.
	– Embed EH&W into the business people strategy.
	– Ensure learning and development resources include EH&W content.
	– Include EH&W support within people policies and processes.
	– With EH&W specialists, support business leaders to prioritise EH&W by reviewing people data, e.g. company-wide culture survey, that includes components of wellbeing, for their part of the business and develop plans to address priority areas.
Facilities	– Ensure that the work environment supports the physical and mental health of employees.
Occupational Health and wellbeing experts	– Develop a data-driven EH&W strategy and gain leadership buy-in to be key sponsors.
	– Provide an effective, high-quality Occupational Health service.
	– Identify the biggest challenges to positive EH&W and provide the most impactful solutions to address them.
	– Develop training material for employees and managers to build their EH&W competencies.
	– Review effectiveness and impact of EH&W services regularly and adapt as necessary.

While it is rare for all eight factors to be present within an organisation, the more that can be embedded, the greater the potential impact on employees and the business.

ACTIONS

1. Develop a comprehensive employee health and wellbeing strategy, with clear goals and plans on how they will be achieved.
2. Integrate employee health and wellbeing into the company people strategy
3. The CEO must regularly communicate their commitments to EH&W, role model positive employee health and wellbeing, champion the EH&W agenda, and set expectations of their executive team to drive the agenda forward, and of all employees to invest in their EH&W.
4. Appoint an executive-level employee health and wellbeing sponsor and a EH&W board to oversee delivery of the strategy.
5. Hold the executive team accountable for driving the employee health and wellbeing agenda through their respective organisations.
6. Map all key stakeholders that play a role in EH&W, gain alignment on the EH&W strategy, and clarify their roles and responsibilities in relation to health and wellbeing while seeking opportunities to integrate efforts. Select and promote line managers on their ability to demonstrate effective EH&W leadership.
7. Activate all levels of the organisation to create a positive culture of health and wellbeing.
8. Measure and track wellbeing metrics, to identify needs, tailor and target interventions, review their impact and adjust approach accordingly and drive leadership accountability.

REFERENCES

CIPD. (2021). *Health and wellbeing at work survey 2021.* London: Chartered Institute of Personnel and Development.

Goetzel, R.Z., & Ozminkowski, R.J. (2008). The health and cost benefits of work site health-promotion programs. *Annual Review of Public Health, 29,* 303–323.

Health Education England. (2019). *NHS Staff and Learners' Mental Wellbeing Commission.* Retrieved, November 20, 2023 from https://www.hee.nhs.uk/sites/default/files/documents/NHS%20%28HEE%29%20-%20Mental%20Wellbeing%20Commission%20Report%20%28Summary%29.pdf

Isham, A., Mair, S., & Jackson, T. (2020). Wellbeing and productivity: A review of the literature. Centre for the Understanding of Sustainable Prosperity. CUSP Working Paper Series. No 22. Guildford: University of Surrey.

McGillivray, D. (2002). Health promotion in the workplace: A missed opportunity? *Health Education, 102*(2), 60–67.

3

HEALTH AND WELLBEING MUST BE OWNED BY AND DRIVEN THROUGH BUSINESS LEADERS

Key messages

1. There is often the perception within organisations that the wellbeing of employees is 'owned' by HR. While HR plays a significant role in supporting EH&W, being the custodian of people policies and processes and a close partner to business leaders, ownership of employee wellbeing must, however, sit with business leaders.

2. The quality of line manager–employee relationships, in particular positive line manager support, is one of the strongest predictors of wellbeing. It improves job commitment and retention, while protecting against burnout.

3. When it comes to employee health and wellbeing, the three key roles of a leader are: to invest in their own self-care; to check in with their staff; and to create a culture of trust.

4. Self-care is the regular practice of maintaining our physical, emotional and mental health. Self-care is the foundation of wellbeing, resilience, high performance, and successful leadership. It requires personal effort, external resources, and action from both individuals and the organisation.

5. Physical self-care involves switching off as well as paying attention to our physical activity, sleep and nutrition. Expressing genuine gratitude to staff is a significant motivator and driver of employee satisfaction and performance. Mindfulness-based interventions in the workplace improve stress levels, relationships and productivity and can significantly reduce sickness absence from all causes. For knowledge workers, thoughtful daily scheduling, where energy and

DOI: 10.4324/9781003124979-3

concentration levels are matched to the task type, and minimising multitasking, will enable more efficient and effective working.

6. Leader wellbeing affects not only their own wellbeing, but also that of those they lead, highlighting the impact of role- modelling self-care. Manager self-care must therefore be part of the strategy to promote the wellbeing of all individuals within an organisation. Placing emphasis on investing in self-care across all levels of an organisation (not only managers) signals the importance an organisation gives to positive wellbeing. Individuals must be given the opportunity to engage with self-care during the workday, wherever possible.

7. Leader wellbeing is a driver of leadership effectiveness. It should be considered a core leadership competency and positioned and prioritised as a critical component of leadership development.

8. Greater attention to leader selection, development, evaluation, and feedback in relation to how they support employee wellbeing will enable successful cultural change and positive employee experience.

9. Checking in regularly with those whom we manage creates a climate of psychosocial safety, at the individual and team level, mitigates against adverse effects of high-intensity work, and positively impacts individual wellbeing and team performance. This is through enabling people to open up and be themselves. Senior leaders must ensure that line managers have the motivation, skills and opportunity to support their teams effectively. They must provide clarity on the expectations of them in relation to employee wellbeing, while holding them to account to deliver. Leadership compassion and vulnerability help create cultures of trust.

10. Organisations must provide line manager training to enable leaders to better support their employees. Training should involve building skills in self-care, how to have a meaningful conversation and take appropriate action, building compassion and spotting the signs of poor wellbeing. Positioning training as mandatory will result in a consistent approach across the organisation. Additional support, such as line manager access to coaching, mentoring and peer networks, will enable managers to prioritise and embed wellbeing practices while learning together.

11. A major caveat is that promoting resilience through self-care must be balanced with identifying and eliminating potential workplace factors that may be driving work stress and impacting productivity. Without addressing these root cause, attempts to build resilience resilience will have limited impact.

INTRODUCTION

HR plays a critical role in integrating EH&W into people policies and processes and influencing business leaders to embed EH&W into how they run their business. It is not uncommon within organisational structures, for the health and wellbeing team to report into HR (or Safety teams, in organisations that have significant safety risks that require a sizeable Safety organisation). While HR plays a part in ensuring there is the right H&W expertise to support the business in managing key health and wellbeing risks, ownership for EH&W lies firmly with business leaders and line managers. This is an important distinction to make and clarify with business leaders so that they are clear on their roles and responsibilities when it comes to the health and wellbeing of the people they lead and manage. (Chapter 6 explores EH&W expertise in more detail.)

IMPACT OF LINE MANAGEMENT EXPERIENCES ON EMPLOYEE HEALTH AND WELLBEING

The single biggest influence on the health and wellbeing of employees at work (and often outside of it) is their relationship with their line manager. For instance, receiving positive support from one's line manager is one of the strongest predictors of wellbeing (Myers, 2003). There is a direct link between how employees relate to their managers and how they feel, physically and mentally, not just while at work but also later in life. A sobering finding in a large-scale study of over 3000 employees showed a strong link between leadership behaviour and heart disease in employees (Nyberg et al., 2009). Perceived poor managerial leadership, expressed as displeasure with their managers at the start of the study, increased not only the amount of sick leave taken at a workplace, but also the risk of sickness amongst employees later in life. In fact, the longer a person had a 'poorer' manager, the higher his or her risk of, for example, suffering a heart attack within a ten-year period. Conversely, support within a climate of trust promotes good relationships between employees and managers, which in turn leads to high levels of employee wellbeing (Baptiste, 2008). In fact, perceived positive managerial support has been associated with a reduction in burnout risk and other negative health-related issues

(Thompson & Prottas, 2006). It is widely acknowledged that people leave managers and not companies. Having a supportive line manager is critical, not only for the wellbeing of employees, but, additionally, for job satisfaction, commitment to the organisation, and whether they decide to stay in the job (Arnold, 2017). Within most workplaces today, the amount and pace of work is increasing, resulting in negative consequences for wellbeing. A survey of 315 workers in a lean manufacturing plant showed that work intensification is transmitted into poorer wellbeing through greater emotional exhaustion. This was, however, buffered by line-manager support. This study suggests that the health-impairing risks of high work intensity in lean settings can be reduced through better supervisory support (Huo et al., 2022). Addressing the root causes of is, of course, vital.

Studies on healthcare workers dealing with previous infectious disease outbreaks highlight the powerful effect that supportive managers have on the mental health of their staff (Brooks et al., 2018). More recently, a study was conducted to look at the impact of Covid-19 on the mental health and wellbeing of rural paramedics, police, community nursing and child protection staff in Australia (Roberts et al., 2021). Mean depression and anxiety scores were around 2–3 times that found in the general community. Over half (56.1%) of respondents showed high emotional exhaustion (burnout). A significant proportion of respondents were seriously considering quitting (27.4%) or looking for a new job with a different employer (28.5%) in the next 12 months. Support from management was significantly associated with better scores on all mental health outcome variables. This emphasises the value of empowering and equipping managers to respond to and address local team needs as they arise. Enhancing line manager support should be a key focus area within all organisations and will be covered later in this chapter.

The 'NHS check' study looking at the impact of the Covid-19 pandemic on the mental health of over 4000 healthcare workers found that, despite experiencing substantial mental health challenges, only half of NHS staff felt supported by their managers and 11% felt not at all supported by their supervisors or managers (Lamb et al., 2021). These observations are a call for organisations to do more to enable all their line managers to support their staff, such as educating managers on their role and providing them with the necessary skills and space needed to execute this aspect of their role. Senior leaders have a role in setting and communicating these expectations and holding line managers to account to deliver them. Many organisations go to the effort of offering high-quality manager training; however, disappointingly, the uptake, which is often voluntary, is rather low and therefore the potential impact, on both the individual and the organisation, is suboptimal. Considering the importance and effectiveness of line manager training, organisations would be well placed to position this as a mandatory or expected foundational line manager core competency.

SUEZ recycling and recovery UK employs more than 5600 people, operating across hundreds of sites, and handles in excess of 10 million tonnes of waste materials every year – a significant proportion of the UK's total waste. Through collection, treatment, recycling and logistics operations, it serves more than 30,000 business customers and millions of householders throughout the country. This example illustrates how SUEZ recycling and recovery UK encourages managers to have meaningful conversations, by providing training and holding them to account through their performance development review process.

The Role of the Manager – SUEZ recycling and recovery UK.

Dr Tracey Leghorn – Chief Business Services Officer and Natalie Sáenz, SW Regional Communications Manager

In 2022 we introduced a wellbeing and inclusion personal bonusable objective (PBO) for all graded employees, helping to drive the importance of wellbeing and inclusion within our business. They had to complete unconscious bias training and organise an activity for their team that supported wellbeing and inclusion in some way. We also included a question about wellbeing in our performance development review (PDR) process; this was to encourage manager-led conversations around wellbeing. We also asked managers to support the release of 10 operational employees from each region to join our Wellbeing and Inclusion Conference held in Manchester. In collaboration with our external mental health specialist, we produced an interactive manager's guide to wellbeing to help support them in conversations around wellbeing and mental health. We have committed to train, over the next three years, all managers, with direct reports in first aid for mental health.

THE THREE KEY ROLES OF THE LINE MANAGER IN EMPLOYEE HEALTH AND WELLBEING

Roles of the Line Manager

Figure 3.1 The key roles of the line manager in workplace health and wellbeing

Self-care

The compelling case for self-care

There is increasing recognition that those in leadership roles are taking in, and being adversely impacted by, the stress of the people they manage. Consideration of wellbeing must extend to leaders, who are likely, under significant pressures, to look after their business and teams to the detriment of their own wellbeing.

Self-care is the regular practice of taking care of our physical, emotional, and mental health. Self-care is often at the bottom of a line manager's list; however, there are many reasons why it needs to be at the top.

INCREASED RESILIENCE AND REDUCED LIKELIHOOD OF BURNOUT

Self-care practices, implemented regularly, serve as coping mechanisms to decrease the impact of high levels of stress, while also serving as strategies for coping during particularly stressful times.

Our daily lives are filled with demands on our energy and time. To meet these demands we need to ensure we have sufficient capacity. For instance, we cannot work at full capacity throughout the working day without taking regular breaks. Individuals who are unable to counterbalance the expenditure of personal resources at work with resource gain or recovery are at risk for burnout (Gorgievski & Hobfoll, 2008). Burnout is now included in the 11th Revision of the International Classification of Diseases (ICD-11) as an occupational phenomenon (World Health Organization, 2019). Burnout is a syndrome conceptualised as resulting from chronic workplace stress that has not been successfully managed. Work–related stress has been defined as a harmful reaction that people have to undue pressures and demands placed on them at work (Health and Safety Executive, n.d.-a). Burnout is characterised by three dimensions: feelings of energy depletion or exhaustion; increased mental distance from one's job; or feelings of negativism or cynicism related to one's job, and reduced professional efficacy. Burnout may impact performance and is associated with decreased productivity. For instance, in healthcare, physician burnout has been associated with lower patient satisfaction and longer post-discharge recovery time (Halbesleben & Rathert, 2008).

Conversely, resilience protects against burnout. The American Psychological Association (2014) defines resilience as "the process of adapting well in the face of adversity, trauma, tragedy, threats or even significant sources of stress". Resilience refers to positive adaptation, or the ability to maintain or regain mental health, despite experiencing adversity (Wald et al., 2006). Those possessing high levels of resilience are said to display a greater capacity to cope with stressful work demands in comparison to other employees (Winwood et al., 2013). Resilience has been positively related to job satisfaction (Zheng et al., 2017). It protects against depression, absence and productivity when job strain is high (Shatté et al., 2017).

Resilience is enhanced through self-care practices. A survey conducted on medical students measured self-care, perceived stress, and quality of life. Self-care moderated the relationship between stress and psychological and physical quality of life in medical students (Ayala et al., 2018).

While some people are more resilient than others, rather encouragingly, we all have the capacity to build resilience, which can be developed over time through training (Howe et al., 2012), something which should be high up on the organisational agenda. With burnout being a significant risk to personal health and business success, self-care must take priority.

The following is an example of leadership development focussed on self-care at Wrightington Wigan and Leigh Teaching Hospitals NHS Foundation Trust.

Wrightington Wigan and Leigh Teaching Hospitals NHS Foundation Trust.

Zoe Garnett – Staff Wellbeing Manager

We are currently developing a training resource for our leaders around wellbeing which will be part of the onboarding process for new leaders and an element of core learning for our existing leaders at all levels of the organisation. This resource will cover the 4 key elements of our Steps4Wellness offer – physical health, mental health, healthy choices and keeping social – and what this means for them as leaders of the team in terms of supporting team colleagues, a part of which will involve facilitating supportive wellbeing conversations with them. Part of the training will cover aspects of their own wellbeing and resilience as leaders at the Trust as well as signposting leaders to avenues of further wellbeing support for themselves and their team colleagues.

ENHANCED LEADERSHIP EFFECTIVENESS

A leader's own wellbeing and self-care behaviours are associated with the self-care and wellbeing habits of those they supervise, through wellbeing role modelling. For instance, less burnout was experienced by US military medical staff members in Afghanistan when their leaders advocated health-promoting behaviours (Adler et al., 2017). These findings build the case for training leaders to engage in behaviours that balance promoting business priorities, in this case the medical priorities of the mission, and ensuring individuals take care of themselves physically and psychologically. In addition to the positive shadow that is cast when leaders self-care, they are also rated as more effective leaders by their employees when they self-care. To demonstrate this relationship, a survey study at Stanford University

School of Medicine on 57 physician leaders and the 820 physicians they supervised found that professional fulfilment and self-care practices of physician leaders were associated with their independently assessed leadership effectiveness (Shanafelt et al., 2020). The authors concluded that training, skill building, and support to improve leader wellbeing should be considered dimensions of leadership development that enhance leader effectiveness (rather than simply a dimension of self-care). Positioned this way, self-care is more likely to better motivate leaders into action. Leader wellbeing should therefore be a core component of organisational leadership development.

PERFORMANCE IMPROVEMENTS

In addition to benefits to mental wellbeing, self-care improves performance. For instance, nurses who completed a behavioural intervention that focused on enhancing self-regulation of the physiological aspects of the stress response showed significant improvements not only to self-reported motivation, anxiety, depression, stress symptoms, but also to productivity from baseline to 7-month follow-up (Pipe et al., 2012). Similarly, newly qualified police officers receiving imagery and relaxation training over an 11-week period went on to display lower stress levels and lower negative mood in comparison to a control group who did not receive the training. Those who received the training were also judged to have superior performance on a critical incident simulation by an independent police officer (Arnetz et al., 2009).

Caveat

The term resilience can have negative connotations. A common misconception associated with 'resilience' is that the onus is on the individual, and, therefore, sending employees on resilience or stress management programmes can often be regarded as having addressed the issue. While individual interventions such as these have impact, they must be balanced with organisational-level interventions. 'Resilience' as a concept should be used with caution for its focus on individual-level rather than structural-level factors (Fletcher & Sarkar, 2013). Both aspects warrant attention. Having a supportive manager, employee social networks and social support structures, identifying the root cause of employee stress and addressing these are important determinants of resilience and emphasise the role organisations and managers play, in addition to individual actions.

Putting self-care into practice

Self-care means different things to different people. Essentially, it is doing what you need to do during and outside the working day to be at your best at work and at home.

Self-care can be divided into physical, mental and emotional dimensions; however, self-care need not require three separate actions. Often, a single activity can support more than one, and often all dimensions. For instance, physical activity, such as going for a walk or run, can support all three dimensions through increasing bloodflow to our brain and muscle cells. This means we can experience greater physical energy, enhanced mental focus and a calmer and more positive outlook.

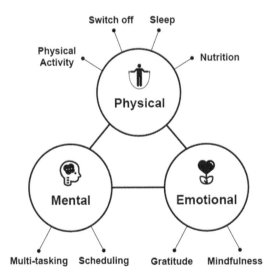

Figure 3.2 The dimensions of self-care

The physical dimension

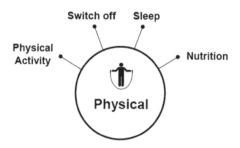

Figure 3.3 The physical dimension of self-care

Physical activity

Physical inactivity increases the risk of developing chronic diseases (Hallal et al., 2012). Being physically active is undoubtedly good for us. Irrespective, however, of the amount of physical activity we engage in, total sitting time is associated with greater risk for several major chronic disease outcomes, and above the threshold of 6–8 h/day of total sitting time, the death rate from all causes of death for a population in a given time period is increased (Patterson et al., 2018)

Restrictions during the Covid-19 pandemic increased our sedentary time. An international study predominantly across Asia, Africa and Europe looking at the behavioural and lifestyle consequences of Covid-19 restrictions. Ammar et al. (2020) found that Covid-19 home confinement had a negative effect on all physical activity intensity levels (vigorous, moderate, walking and overall). Additionally, daily sitting time increased more than 28% from 5 to 8 h per day and the proportion of individuals who sat for more than 8 h a day increased from 16% to 40% during confinement.

Exercise plays a significant role in improving mental health (Stathopoulou et al., 2006). A workplace study on employees in the private and public sectors found that workday exercise can improve mood and self-reported performance of office workers on days when they exercise at work over days when they do not (Coulson et al., 2008). Even low-intensity activities such as walking significantly increases creative thinking (Oppezzo & Schwartz, 2014) and spending time in nature positively impacts mental health (Kotera et al., 2020).

Even short periods of physical activity, such as 10 minutes, have shown to improve fatigue and mood (Hansen et al., 2001).

Amongst office workers, standing for part of the day has proven physical short- and long-term health benefits (Buckley et al., 2014). When comparing sitting to standing desk-based workers, those who stood to carry out their work after lunch had greater energy expenditure and better blood glucose control, highlighting why avoiding sedentary behaviour at work could lead to a reduced risk of cardio-metabolic diseases.

Those who have more sedentary roles should be encouraged to move more throughout the day. For instance, promoting stretching at the desk, meetings while standing or walking, where conditions allow, and short periods of movement interspersed throughout the day. The following is an example, at British Telecom, of a motivational campaign to increase physical activity. Involving managers as key sponsors and contributing to charity were key success factors in encouraging uptake:

British Telecom – The big stretch.

Dr Richard Caddis – Director of Health & Wellbeing and Chief Medical Officer, BT Group

To help employees form new healthy habits, the 'big stretch' campaign was launched to stretch employees by challenging them to enhance their physical and mental wellbeing. Employees were asked to sign up to a physical health commitment and one other wellbeing goal on their 'fit for life' platform and managers were supported to become coaches and role models for this initiative and were positioned as critical to its success. To gain traction, BT committed to donating to names charity partners for each sign up so that employees not only got healthier but in doing so supported communities. Participants were encouraged to share posts on their progress and engage in wider wellbeing activities as well as physical, such as mindfulness, learning and giving.

To support increased physical activity, organisations can offer a variety of options such as sit-stand desks, bike access, walking paths, on-site fitness centres or subsidies to local ones, online or app-based fitness class access, desk exercise aids.

Switch off

Switching off, which can be considered as recovery, is protective against work-related stress and increases physical and psychological wellbeing. It enables a healthy work–life balance.

Chronically working long hours is generally associated with lower wellbeing through impeding our ability to recover (Bryan & Nandi, 2015). It is of no surprise then that workers are most engaged during workdays preceded by evenings when workers have recovered well (Sonnentag, 2003); however, quality of recovery is hindered when we find it difficult to relax at home after a stressful working day. When workers worry in their private time about the past or upcoming working day, it impedes the recovery process (Brosschot et al., 2005). Adequate recovery, on the other hand, allows us to balance the expenditure of personal resources at work with resource gain or recovery and thereby sustain our capacity to meet the demands of work. Leisure time is important for recuperation from work stress and can be considered an important determinant of health and wellbeing (Rook & Zijlstra, 2006).

There is a perception (and common practice) among many that recovery needs to wait until the weekend or a holiday; however, investing in recovery in the workday is just as, if not more, important. Workers are most engaged during workdays when they have access to a variety of resources and daily recovery (Bakker, 2014). As an example, a randomised controlled study found that a four-week respite intervention helped employees replenish and build energy resources at work (Steidle et al., 2017). Taking part in either a daily simulated savouring nature intervention or a progressive muscle relaxation intervention resulted in more stable energy levels after the intervention period, demonstrating the impact of recovery interventions. Regardless of the specific practice, the key message here is to regularly engage in an activity. We all have unique ways to switch off, including going for a walk or run, practising yoga or mindfulness, connecting with someone, reading, socialising, good-quality sleep, and doing the things we enjoy, all of which support recovery. Enabling employees to switch off through means that work best for them will motivate them to invest in their personal recovery and renewal, supporting them to be at their best in the workplace and at home. Workday recovery is clearly more possible for office-based workers; however, roles where there is less personal freedom for this, such as those in manufacturing, sales, construction or healthcare, can be supported though measures such as ensuring healthy shift patterns and adequate recovery breaks and providing education, physical space and resources for recovery. These employee groups are likely unable to have the choice to take a day, or even a few hours out of their workday to attend self-care workshops. Employers will therefore need to be creative in how content is delivered to them, for instance, through breaking up content into small bite-sized chunks, to be delivered as part of their regular operational team meetings over several months rather than on one day. Supervisors who are passionate advocates of wellbeing can be trained to deliver the content. This will ensure all employees, irrespective of role, have access to practical ways to self-care.

Sleep

Our sleep is strongly linked to our physical, mental and emotional health. Insufficient sleep has been associated with cognitive problems, reduced job performance, decreased motivation, and increased safety risks. There have been several studies concluding that failure to get adequate sleep contributes to medical errors (Baldwin & Daugherty, 2004). Previous studies have found a link between a leader's sleep health and leadership effectiveness through an effect on the leader's relationships with team members (Guarana & Barnes, 2017).

Sleep helps us to adapt and cope with challenges. Our sleep was adversely affected during the pandemic (Xue et al., 2020). Data from 46,284 UK adults in the Covid-19 Social Study assessed weekly from 01/04/2020 to 12/05/2020 was analysed to study the association between life adversities and sleep quality (Wright et al., 2021). Six categories of adversity were looked at, including both worries and experiences of: illness with Covid-19, financial difficulty, loss of paid work, difficulties acquiring medication, difficulties accessing food, and threats to personal safety. All worries and experiences were significantly related to poorer-quality sleep, except experiences relating to employment and finances. Having a larger social network offered some buffering effects. The authors concluded that poor sleep may be a mechanism by which Covid-19 adversities affected mental health. This study provides a strong case for offering sleep interventions in the workplace to help people cope, beyond the pandemic. A large body of literature further supports the positive association between social support and better sleep (Kent et al., 2018). It appears that improved sleep has been identified as a pathway through which social support may affect health (Nordin et al., 2008). This reinforces the advantage of greater employee connections and network building and the role that organisations should play in driving connectivity, to improve sleep and its positive knock-on effects.

Helping employees have better quality and quantity of sleep is an investment that will pay dividends. Supporting employees to better manage stress, improve social connections and provide education on how to improve their sleep, should be core components of health promotion efforts. (Chapter 6 contains a sleep and a fatigue case study.)

Nutrition

There is increasing appetite, in the workplace, for introducing dietary interventions, to help employees lead healthier lifestyles. Workplace nutritional improvement efforts can positively influence diet and health outcomes (Schliemann & Woodside, 2019) and therefore the workplace is an ideal environment to influence healthy eating. People with a poor diet who are overweight are more likely to suffer from absenteeism (Cancelliere, et al., 2011) and, therefore, dietary interventions may result in cost savings due to reducing absenteeism. Our diet also influences our performance and interactions. What we eat, when we eat and how much we eat impacts our performance, for instance, through affecting our energy levels, concentration, cognitive function and the quality of interaction with others. Trying to change several dietary elements at once can be overwhelming and therefore campaigns directed at encouraging employees to focus on one aspect of their diet at a time may be more impactful. An example is increasing dietary intake of fruits and vegetables which is associated with greater eudaemonic well-being (a state of flourishing characterised by feelings of engagement, meaning, and purpose in life) and greater curiosity and creativity (Conner et al., 2015).

Interventions that are the most effective include both those that improve employee education and ones that make positive environmental changes (e.g., healthier food availability, subsidising healthy food, food labelling). Making the nutritional intervention part of a comprehensive programme of healthy lifestyle changes will ensure a systematic, holistic and more impactful and sustainable approach.

Frontline workers can be the hardest to reach but the most in need of support. The following example shows how SUEZ recycling and recovery UK reaches their frontline workers through taking a multi-pronged approach that supported healthier dietary habits. Similar approaches can be taken by organisations that employ a significant proportion of non-office-based workers.

SUEZ recycling and recovery UK.

Dr Tracey Leghorn, Chief Business Services Officer, and Natalie Sáenz, SW Regional Communications Manager

SUEZ runs webinars on eating for wellbeing and 'Know your numbers' and we educate our employees on how diet can support their health (cholesterol/high blood pressure). Our employee benefit platform You@SUEZ has a host of healthy step-by-step recipes for employees to access and follow. We produce flyers on healthy nutrition, in collaboration with our occupational health providers which are shared at site level. We ran a Health and Wellbeing roadshow where lifestyle and diet are discussed (6 different sites per year). This year's wellbeing and inclusion conference has a morning feature around diet and wellbeing with a cooking demonstration from Kumud Ghandi and a Q&A about eating for immunity. 70% of attendees are operational employees.

The emotional dimension

Figure 3.4 The emotional dimension of self-care

Consciously managing our emotions enables us to operate at our best emotional state. Positive emotions enhance not only our wellbeing, resulting in us feeing good, but also boost creativity, critical thinking processes and performance. Positive psychology brings a wealth of research on the development of resilience (Tugade & Fredrickson, 2004). Two practices that have been proven to build resilience and enhance performance at work are gratitude and mindfulness.

Gratitude

We all respond positively to being appreciated. Gratitude has both personal and organisational value. Individuals with a high degree of gratitude tend to experience lower stress, which then, in turn, increases their satisfaction with life (Yildirim & Alanazi, 2018). Gratitude protects people from stress and depression (Wood et al., 2008). Practising gratitude has been shown to be a predictor of job performance and job satisfaction (Cortini et al., 2019) and enhances collaboration between co-workers (Wood et al., 2008). Managers who show meaningful ways to appreciate their staff will see high levels of organisational and leader commitment, higher levels of engagement and lower turnover rates. Gratitude is relatively simple to implement, yet not practised enough in the workplace. Gratitude can take many forms, such as appreciating the work of others directly to them and/or in the presence of others, journalling reasons to be grateful, starting a team meeting with each member sharing one thing they are grateful for and regularly celebrating team successes. Expressing gratitude must be genuine and specific, such as highlighting the behaviour observed or experienced rather than a generic "well done" statement.

Mindfulness

In 1979, Jon Kabat-Zinn developed an eight-week stress-reduction programme, which we now call Mindfulness-Based Stress Reduction (MBSR). Since then, a mounting body of research has demonstrated how mindfulness-based interventions improve mental and physical health. According to Kabat-Zinn, mindfulness is awareness that arises through paying attention, on purpose, in the present moment, non-judgementally. Individual coping strategies, such as acceptance, behavioural activation and mindfulness, are thought to be particularly effective during crises or disasters as they foster resilience and recovery (Polizzi et al., 2020). People who practice mindfulness are less stressed (Jensen, et al., 2015), sleep better (Winbush et al., 2007), are better able to concentrate and sustain attention on tasks (MacLean et al., 2010) and are more creative (Ostafin & Kassman, 2012).

As the Covid-19 pandemic demonstrated, demands placed on human service workers in supporting people through challenging circumstances contributed to high levels of stress and burnout. (Chapter 4 highlights the challenges workers faced within the health and social care sector.) Among human service workers, contemplative practices, including mindfulness, have been shown to improve awareness (which enhances coping), and self-care preventative practices, within approximately eight weeks. While mindfulness significantly increased, stress significantly decreased over the intervention, which positively impacted workers and their clients (McGarrigle & Walsh, 2011). In a study on frontline healthcare professionals during the Covid-19 outbreak, 5–10 minutes of mindfulness practices were delivered twice daily by experienced psychiatrists, psychologists, and mental health nurses. As a result, approximately half of the nurses found that brief mindfulness sessions on site were helpful for reducing stress, with a mean rating of 8.4 on a scale from 0 to 10. (Rodriguez-Vega et al., 2020). In another study on nurses, a mindfulness intervention aimed to develop internal self-awareness, emotional intelligence, and enhance team relationships, through maintaining connection and appreciation of others. Results demonstrated improved job satisfaction and reduced burnout risks (Monroe et al., 2021).

As a result of a growingly robust evidence base, mindfulness in the workplace is gaining traction. Many organisations provide access to mindfulness classes, covering topics including dealing with change, uncertainly, emotions, and stress. Time, permission, and a place for learning and practicing mindfulness-based activities are key enabling factors and need to be considered as fundamental components of successful implementation of any programme. Simple interventions can have significant personal and business impact. For instance, a six-week stress reduction workshop offered by Transport for London, which taught mindfulness alongside psychological education and cognitive behavioural therapy, demonstrated benefits in terms of well-being and productivity. Among employees who attended the course, the number of absence days due to stress, anxiety and depression had fallen by 71% over the following three years. Absences for all conditions dropped by 50% over that time. In addition, 80% of attendees reported improvements in their relationships, 64% improvements in sleep patterns, and 53% improvements in happiness when at work (Halliwell, 2010). To conclude, gratitude and mindfulness should be included in an organisation's manager development portfolio.

The mental dimension

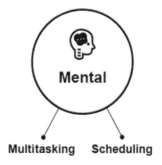

Figure 3.5 The mental dimension of self-care

Multitasking

Multitasking is when we attempt to perform two or more tasks concurrently. It typically leads to repeatedly switching between tasks or leaving one task unfinished, in order to work on another. Multitasking may seem, in theory, to allow us to be more efficient and effective, through being able to do many jobs at the same time. Indeed, certain workplaces or sectors may even recruit based on the ability of the potential employee to multitask. However, studies are discovering that multitasking has negative consequences on productivity, error rate, critical thinking skills, and concentration. Multitasking impacts the individual with regard to stress and can impact relationships (Crews & Russ, 2012). For instance, typing an e-mail while talking to a colleague would be interpreted as not caring enough to give them your full attention. In a study on multitasking in knowledge-intensive business services, employees were strongly engaged in multitasking activities in their workplaces. Most respondents (above 70%) admitted that they were able to make good decisions and concentrate better when they worked on one task at a time (Suija-Markova et al., 2020). Individuals almost always take longer to complete a task and do so with more errors when switching between tasks than when they stay with one task (Madore & Wagner, 2019). When it comes to learning, people have a harder time learning new things when their brains are distracted by another activity (Poldrack & Foerde, 2007) as learning while distracted or multitasking, alters the brain's learning processes. Additionally, when information is obtained under multitasking conditions, the flexible application of knowledge associated with creativity and adaptive problem solving may be less likely to occur.

Considering the adverse effects on stress, relationships and performance, employers must find ways to discourage multitasking in the workplace, where possible.

Ways to practically reduce multitasking:

- Focus your attention on one task at a time rather than flipping from one task to another.
- Minimise distractions. Turn off your phone and e-mail alerts and notifications. Schedule e-mail time into your diary rather than interrupting work to answer e-mails as they come in.
- Tech-free meeting rule, unless necessary in a meeting.

Scheduling

Taking time to plan our day, week and even month can seem too time-consuming compared to being on autopilot, yet it can make a big difference to how effective we are.

- Schedule tasks to align your work activities with your energy levels. E.g., when you are most alert, complete tasks needing your full attention, creativity or complex thinking and conduct routine tasks (e.g., responding to routine e-mails) when energy levels may not be at their highest.

- Schedule breaks, however small, into your workday to renew energy and concentration levels.
- If possible, rotate between sitting and standing during the workday and talk while walking, if looking at a screen is not needed.
- Consider the best time to hold your one-to-one meetings. For instance, if you need to complete a task needing focus and attention and are most alert in the mornings, schedule one-to-one meetings in the afternoons.

Putting self-care into practice

The following is an example from British Telecom on how to develop and promote a sustainable self-care programme, to help employees enhance their wellbeing.

British Telecom – recharge your wellbeing campaign.

Dr Ricards Caddis – Director of Health & Wellbeing and Chief Medical Officer, BT Group

An evidence-based 28-day programme of daily activities was designed internally to enable participants to regain or build their wellbeing as part of the recovery from the pandemic and to help get employees back into the workplace with higher levels of wellbeing. This was conceived, designed, and developed from scratch. It was put together in a new way using video and a combination of methodologies to ensure high user participation and ease. It was launched as a campaign but constructed in such a way that it did not become constrained to use just during the pandemic but could be used at any time. So far have 'relaunched' the programme three times by 're-booting' or 'revitalising'.

Key principles were to create a programme that would be fun and challenging to help us 'recharge' our wellbeing and enable us to be better equipped to deal with whatever is round the corner. The programme runs for 28 days in order to help develop and embed healthy habits. The activities and exercises are drawn from science and designed to be achievable whatever level of fitness or health employees are currently experiencing. The 'recharge' programme will build from the successful Five Ways to Wellbeing approach developed by the New Economic Foundation and adopted by the UK NHS. It is supported by access to expert coaches, video guides, weekly live forums, e-mail nudges, access to supportive workplace community of participants, and simple-to-follow activities. Additionally, there are optional modules to support the programme and follow on modules after the programme concludes.

The first campaign (2022) was received extremely well and there were numerous bouquets and unsolicited thanks. The second campaign (2023) we tracked the number of registrations and we had over 1800 employees register. At the time of updating this (2024), we have had over 3400 employees register and we are only in the first week of registrations.

Success factors for self-care

While the idea of self-care sounds good on paper, competing demands can mean it remains theoretical, unless prioritised. Practical ways in which self-care can become embedded at the individual and organisational levels include:

Individual

1. **Microbursts (mini-breaks)**. Despite the benefits of self-care, most of us do not prioritise this, believing we do not have the time. Self-care, however, does not require long periods of time out but rather short bursts of a few minutes, practiced frequently. Strategies to build energy into your day include setting calendar meetings to default to 25 and 50 minutes, using the remaining 5 or 10 minutes to recover, blocking calendar time for breaks, if able to do so, scheduling breaks, however short, to renew energy e.g., a short walk/stretching/getting a drink or snack/journaling/watching a TED talk/taking deep breaths. Ten minutes of physical activity is easier to commit to than trying to find an hour in your day to recover, and will provide physical and mental health benefits.
2. **Regularity**. Building self-care into your daily practice will form long-term habits that can be woven naturally into the course of your workday. This requires planning and discipline, in service of energy renewal.

Organisational

3. **Executive support and advocacy**. Engaging in self-care is easier when there is sponsorship and role modelling from the top, to encourage teams towards healthy behaviours. Senior leaders who communicate what they do to self-care and set expectations of others to do so will send strong motivational signals to act.

4. **Self-care role models** across all levels of the organisation can act as catalysts to activate change.

5. **Offer training to develop personal self-care**. Training on how to tap into the state of our physical, emotional and mental health, on building energy capacity and resilience, will enable us to better meet demands, and bounce back when encountering challenging times. Creating the opportunity for staff to attend training during the working day will maximise uptake. UK Policing offers manager training, seeking regular feedback to keep it relevant to the needs of their staff:

UK Policing – Manager training.

Andy Rhodes and Dr Ian Hesketh

National Police Wellbeing Service (NPWS) engages at every level of leadership, providing training and guidance. This includes high-quality peer training, trauma intervention training and online resources in areas such as sleep and mindfulness. We have a very close working relationship with police and police staff associations. This is because they provide vital support. We schedule regularly meets with these key stakeholders to ensure we are not duplicating effort and to share knowledge, good and promising practice.

---

6. **Sustaining self-care though coaching and mentoring**. Coaching can help embed learned behaviours that training has imparted, through supporting employees and managers to continue to invest in their wellbeing. It can be delivered successfully within a group or one-to-one setting, either virtually or face to face. Mentors are often selected to support performance development. Choosing a mentor who effectively balances this with self-care and is a positive role model for wellbeing, will support line

manager development in self and team wellbeing, team engagement and, ultimately, performance. This type of mentor can also champion wellbeing in broader forums such as townhalls.

7. **Leverage Technology**. Technology can be used to scale EH&W messaging and resources, to cast the net wider, reaching more employees. The market is saturated with wellbeing apps to support self-care. Provided only those with a strong evidence base are selected, results can be impressive. A study on military healthcare workers demonstrated the benefits of using technology and mobile phone applications to enhance self-awareness and build resiliency (Lester et al. 2015). Access to apps alone, however, is not enough. They also found that effectiveness of this form of education and training is enhanced when employees are able to work in stable environments, with adequate resources, leadership support, and reasonable workloads.

The John Lewis Partnership is the UK's largest employee owned business and parent company of their two retail brands, John Lewis and Waitrose, which are owned in Trust by over 74,000 Partners. John Lewis & Partners, commonly known as John Lewis, is a British chain of high-end department stores operating across the United Kingdom, with concessions in Ireland. Waitrose & Partners is a British supermarket chain with shops across Great Britain and the Channel Islands. The following is an example of how John Lewis successfully implemented wellbeing technology to support their workforce:

John Lewis – Positive Psychology and self-determination/ self-management.

Nick Davison – former head of Associate Wellbeing

The John Lewis Partnership has a long history of investing in the health and wellbeing of its Partners (employees). Traditionally, this has been focused on rehabilitation support and in leisure and social activities. Prior to the outbreak of the Covid-19 pandemic the benefits of developing a scalable, proactive approach to helping employees develop a positive mindset and equip them to self-manage was recognised.

The Partnership provides free access to a digital tool which combines education and self-help tools across a range of psychological and life stage areas. Whilst individuals use the tools confidentially, the aggregated data enables the Partnership to track aspects of sentiment, participation and measurable improvement from learning.

The uncertainty brought upon by Covid-19 provided an ideal opportunity for the platform to be used to reach those in need of remote support but also to provide tailored content specific to the pandemic.

At the beginning of the pandemic use of the digital tool rose quickly, by over 20%, to 11,000 Partners. The Partnership was able to track Partner sentiment across the months that followed. In March 2020, there was an initial drop across all data points. The sense of Connection remained the strongest but levels of anxiety, fulfilment and the impact of sleep were recorded at lower levels. However, after a two-month period, the pre-Covid-19 levels returned across all of the six areas (Connection, Fulfillment, Calmness, Happiness, Sleep, Health) and have remained consistent through the rest of the pandemic.

The most popular educational series introduced was "Navigating COVID19" followed by "Building Resilience" and "Growing Through Challenging Times". The "Introduction to Mental Health" "Menopause 101" and "Easing Loneliness" have all been popular additions to the content, which has continued to evolve.

The ambition over time is that Partners will develop their self-management skills and be able to develop greater self-awareness and resilience to deal with whatever life brings their way.

Being clear on the problem you are trying to solve will help decide on the right approach. Enabling employees to self-manage in a scalable way was their motivation for sourcing the tool in the example above. Offering an app in itself may increase awareness and access to health and wellbeing resources. However, to what extent and how it is used along with insights gained will help inform needs, value and next steps. In this case, the Health and Wellbeing team took a proactive approach to measure uptake, workplace sentiment and changes in wellbeing associated with this intervention.

CHECK-IN

Regularly checking in with employees demonstrates care and supports people to be at their best. There are three key fundamentals to checking in with employees:

Check in
Showing genuine concern for the wellbeing of employees

Figure 3.6 The elements of a positive check in

1. Express interest in the wellbeing of your employees

Managers can have a significantly positive influence on employee wellbeing, by regularly checking in with them. The pandemic highlighted that the circumstance of every individual employee is unique and different. Some employees may have adapted well to the new experience while others found it tremendously challenging. Some connected with colleagues, had a healthier work–life balance with better wellbeing overall, while for others, these worsened. Engagement and productivity were greater for some and less for others. These differing experiences highlight the need to understand individual circumstances and take an individual approach, through having open, honest, and supportive conversations. Checking in involves having genuine interest in the wellbeing of employees, through open authentic and meaningful conversations with a broad and holistic approach. While work factors can impact wellbeing, it would be amiss to focus solely on these and leave out influences outside the work environment, which also determine our wellbeing (see the 5 drivers of wellbeing in Chapter 1). Insights gained can help managers respond appropriately and ultimately deepen the employee–manager relationship.

Interestingly, there is individual variation in what managers think constitutes employee wellbeing. Senior managers, for instance, interpret wellbeing in multiple ways depending on the national perspective. In one study, for instance, Finnish managers interpreted employee wellbeing predominantly as a reflection of physical and mental health, while in Scotland managers associated it with the enjoyment of work and its impact on personal life and in Bulgaria it is seen as an appraisal of labour conditions and salary levels (Galabova & McKie, 2013). This emphasises the need for managers to understand the breadth of wellbeing and take an individual approach, to understand the unique wellbeing needs of each person.

Health-oriented leader behaviours are a stronger predictor of employee wellbeing than other leadership styles, through their impact on enhancing self-care behaviour amongst employees and influencing how they manage demands, such as creating a healthy work–life balance (Franke et al., 2014). A caveat to this is that the effectiveness of health-oriented leader behaviour depends on employees' expectations, and is stronger the more such behaviour is expected and desired. To ascertain this requires an open two-way dialogue on expectations and needs, so that managers take an individual approach to wellbeing (Kaluza et al., 2021). Managers should therefore explore the extent to which each employee wishes to focus on wellbeing and adapt their approach accordingly. The following case study from Gloucestershire NHS Trust emphasises the power in asking how people are, on a regular basis, to build trust:

Gloucestershire NHS Trust

Chief executive, Deborah Lee, and her Executive Team have made it clear that supporting individuals is part of the day job of a manager, and not a 'bolt-on' or a 'nice to do'. They are asking managers to prioritise employee wellbeing, including their own.

"There is an appreciation that managers have a lot of responsibility and many managers do not feel comfortable to manage employees struggling with their mental health. As a result, the Trust has provided the opportunity for people within teams to undertake training to help with having these conversations."

They found that employees are more likely to open up at team meetings while talking with others on the topic of how they are doing, so at the start of all meetings before going into objective/work mode they start with "How are things for you"? Some meetings never get beyond this!"

2. Identify those with poor wellbeing and act

Practically, managers can offer health-related support and care for employees by noticing health signals and intervening when observing that employees are struggling. A core and fundamental skill for all managers is knowing how to start a supportive conversation with an employee who may be experiencing emotional distress or who opens up about challenges that are impacting their mental health. While some managers handle these situations well, others feel uncomfortable when an employee opens up or shows signs that indicate they are struggling, not knowing what to say, perhaps saying nothing and therefore missing an opportunity to offer timely support to direct the individual towards a path of recovery. Since the pandemic has significantly increased electronic means of communication and, in some cases, minimised face-to-face interactions, managers are exposed to fewer opportunities to tune into the emotions of others and therefore helping managers to identify signs of poor wellbeing and intervene with sensitivity and confidence is critical.

To address any gaps and ensure employees have managers with the necessary skills to help them, organisations are offering training to equip managers with a basic understanding of mental health, including factors that can affect wellbeing. Manager mental health training must include three key elements: gaining practical skills on how to spot the signs of poor wellbeing (including changes in appearance, behaviour and performance); building confidence to step in, reassure and support a person in distress; and acquiring the knowledge of when and how to help someone recover their health by guiding them to further support within and outside the organisation. This is achieved through deepening their interpersonal skills, such as listening non-judgementally, having empathy for others and being open-minded. Supportive wellbeing conversations are part of leadership training at Wrightington Wigan and Leigh Teaching Hospitals NHS Foundation Trust.

Wrightington Wigan and Leigh Teaching Hospitals NHS Foundation Trust.

Zoe Garnett – Staff Wellbeing Manager

We have developed a training resource (training session and toolkit) for leaders at all levels of the organisation, enabling them to have supportive wellbeing conversations with their team members on a regular basis throughout the year to help staff stay healthy and well in work. This resource covers the 4 key elements of our Steps4Wellness offer – physical health, mental health, healthy choices and keeping social – and what this means for them as leaders of the team in terms of having effective wellbeing conversations, supporting team colleagues with their wellbeing, as well as signposting leaders to avenues of further wellbeing support for themselves and their team colleagues.

The following example details the aims, success factors and impact of the line manager mental health training programme within British Telecom:

British Telecom – Managing mental health workshops.

Dr Richard Caddis – Director of Health & Wellbeing and Chief Medical Officer

BT has created a workshop specifically designed for People Managers with the following aims:

- Provide an understanding of mental health issues through increased knowledge and understanding of the major types, symptoms and risk factors associated with common mental health conditions.

- Develop practical skills and confidence in dealing with people affected by these issues appropriately and in a timely manner when managing someone showing signs of declining mental health.
- Introduce a five-step model of safe intervention for managing mental health issues.
- Raise awareness of support available for both manager and individual through informing managers of:
  - Company policies, procedures, programmes, relevant demographics and
  - Resources (internal and external) available.

Success factors

1. The material is tailored for the specific needs of BT.
2. It is delivered by accredited mental health professionals who have an in-depth understanding of the BT organisation and its employees.
3. Various delivery channels are used to maximise access (face to face and virtual).
4. An interactive blend of theory, skills practice, case studies and other learning activities to optimise the learning experience.
5. Using evidence-based reference material from a number of reputable sources working for better mental health, such as the World Health Organisation, the Centre for Mental Health, MIND and the Samaritans.

Feedback

All sessions have extremely high feedback across a range of metrics. A specific follow-up study was undertaken 6 months after course completion by several cohorts of managers. The responses showed that the course was very effective for attendees.

What do the delegates say?

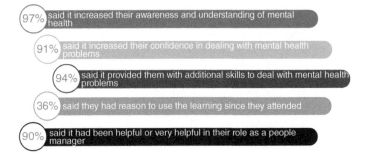

Figure 3.7 British Telecom's 'manager mental health training program' impact

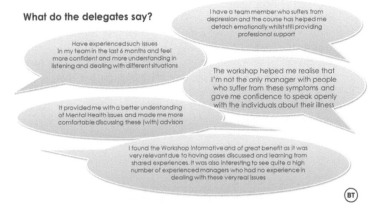

Figure 3.8 British Telecom's 'manager mental health training program' impact

3. Identify and address work stressors

Managers are often reluctant to discuss the possibility of work stress with their employee for fear that this could make the situation worse or create a situation that that they cannot handle. Conversely, however, regularly discussing potential sources of stress will help build trust, enable action to be taken early to prevent chronicity, and positively impact on individual wellbeing and workability. Guidance at the organisational level will ensure consistency in approach.

In the UK, regulatory aspects of mental wellbeing are covered by the Health and Safety Executive's (HSE's) Management Standards (Health and Safety Executive, n.d.-b). The Management of Health and Safety at Work Regulations 1999 require employers to assess the risk of stress-related ill health arising from work activities, as with any other hazard. The Health and Safety at Work Act 1974 requires an employer to take measures to control that risk. These Management Standards cover six key areas of work design that, if not properly managed, are associated with poor health, lower productivity and increased accident and sickness absence rates.

These Management Standards provide a useful checklist for managers, when considering the breadth of possible work stressors. These are defined as:

Demands – includes issues such as workload, work patterns and the work environment.

Control – how much say the person has in the way they do their work.

Support – includes the encouragement, sponsorship and resources provided by the organisation, line management and colleagues.

Relationships – includes promoting positive working to avoid conflict and dealing with unacceptable behaviour.

Role – whether people understand their role within the organisation and whether the organisation ensures that they do not have conflicting roles.

Change – how organisational change (large or small) is managed and communicated in the organisation.

The HSE provides an assessment tool that can be used by organisations to assess these six areas. To effectively implement the Management Standards approach, it is essential for organisations to ensure resource, support, and infrastructure.

These six areas can be useful discussion points in one-to-one check-in conversations, to identify roots causes, if an employee presents with stress. With practice, they can be covered naturally and succinctly.

Making tools available to support managers can facilitate having meaningful conversations. External tools can be used off the shelf or adapted, to reflect the specific work environment.

The following case study demonstrates how these six areas form the basis of an internal stress risk assessment tool at British Telecom, to strengthen psychological risk management. Integrating psychological risk assessment into the role of a line manager is the key to its success.

British Telecom's Stress Assessment Tool (STREAM).

Dr Richard Caddis – Director of Health & Wellbeing and Chief Medical Officer

To ensure compliance with the HSE standards, the BT STREAM assessment tool was developed to support employees and managers to identify and address sources of stress and hold meaningful conversations. The STREAM tool, which stands for 'Stress Assessment and Management', is a self-assessment tool based on HSE's stress management standards. Upon completion of the questions, the tool provides an assessment of personal stress level and highlights areas where the employee may be under stress to help the employee and manager agree on what the employee and BT will do to manage and reduce stress levels. Actual answers are not shared, but overall stress rating and guidance on managing their stress is sent to their first- or second-line manager depending on who the employee choses. An action plan is then co-developed and agreed. The STREAM tool was developed with the consultancy services of a leading psychiatrist from Kings College London and endorsed by the HSE as an appropriate means for identifying stress within their six categories.

The introduction of STREAM achieved a significant number of objectives. Firstly, it exceeded the recommendations of the HSE to address workplace stressors. By providing a report and guidance to both the manager and the employee it facilitated a meaningful conversation to help co-create solutions to the workplace stressors. It also helped raise awareness of the support and services available for both manager and employee. It ensured that the manager recorded the actions taken to enable follow-ups. Anonymised analytics from the reports provided thematic data pointing to where the stressors were prevalent thus informing where to target interventions.

In anticipation of the strengthening of psychological risk management in the workplace, and aligned to ISO 45003, a psychosocial risk assessment has been implemented to enhance the STREAM assessment and formalise the management and review of work design. BT's OH & Wellbeing Centre of Expertise has integrated a psychosocial risk assessment into the everyday role of a people manager. This is a process used to determine if due consideration and reasonable steps have been taken to ensure a role is psychosocially protective for an employee. It forms part of the preventative actions BT takes to ensure all its employees are kept mentally safe at work. With the global psychosocial risk assessment template included in the revised safety manual for the BT group, this will allow for substantial improvements in monitoring and tracking across all business units, thus allowing the BT group to pre-empt and prevent cases of psychosocial absence rather than having problems escalate later.

Create a culture of trust

Consultation and active dialogue between workers and management was crucial throughout the pandemic, to raise concerns and meaningfully engage with workers on any changes in the organisation in addition to challenges they faced. This depended on there being a relationship of trust, where people felt psychologically safe to open up.

The benefits of creating psychological safety

We all have a desire to work in an environment where we can speak openly and be ourselves. Psychological safety is being able to show and employ oneself without fear of negative consequences of self-image, status or career (Kahn, 1990) and many studies have demonstrated a link to healthier and more productive teams. For instance, psychological safety boosts employee engagement (Kark & Carmeli, 2009) and senior team innovation (West & Anderson, 1996). A survey on ambulance personnel across two Australian states found that manager psychosocial safety was a significant predictor of employee mental health (Petrie et al., 2018). An environment of trust is a key determinant of psychological safety (Zhang et al., 2010). When we feel we can trust our manager and colleagues, we are more likely to bring our full selves into the workplace. Consultation and active dialogue between workers and management was been crucial throughout the pandemic, to raise concerns, and meaningfully engage with workers on any changes in the organisation.

How can we create a culture of trust?

Compassion and vulnerability are at the heart of psychological safety, both of which support the development of a climate of trust.

Culture of Trust
Create a psychologically safe space

Figure 3.9 The elements of building a culture of trust

HARNESS COMPASSION

Positive leadership during the Covid-19 pandemic was experienced when leaders and managers expressed empathy, compassion and understanding and demonstrated awareness that their employees' personal circumstances may change rapidly, while responding appropriately (Wu et al., 2020). This holds true today. The act of showing compassion involves being with someone in their pain. It's understanding another's feelings and demonstrating a willingness to act in response to those feelings (Boyatzis, Smith, & Blaize, 2006). Among public service employees, a longitudinal study showed that compassion from supervisors positively predicted future work engagement, organisational citizenship behaviour, client-rated service-oriented performance, and decreased job burnout (Eldor, 2017). Compassionate behaviour has also been associated with increased attachment and commitment to one's organisation (Grant et al., 2008). Nurses achieve improved job performance following experiencing compassion in the workplace, almost completely through the mediating effect of positive moods. In other words, hospital nurses who have experienced more compassion at work tend to have more positive moods and are therefore likely to perform better (Chu, 2016). While for some managers compassion comes easily, it can be developed in others through training. Intervention studies carried out in organisations to foster compassion have included a strong component of mindfulness, such as meditation (Scarlet et al., 2017) and emotional skills training. For instance, a recent study found that compassion is a skill that can be increased among managers through training, to improve emotional skills, with observable benefits for the organisation (Paakkanen et al., 2021). The emotional skills cultivation training developed for this study included elements of compassion, such as noticing, feeling and acting, that alleviate the suffering of another person (Dutton, et al., 2014). Leaders and organisations may benefit from prioritising building compassionate cultures through training and coaching, rewarding compassionate behaviour and by decreasing obstacles to compassion, such as fear of appearing weak if displaying compassion (Gilbert et al., 2011). In fact, successful leaders that role model compassion would serve to challenge this perception, by offering a contrary reality.

The following shows how understanding and implementing an evidence-based approach to wellbeing, demonstrating compassion, empathy and exercising less judgement made a significant cultural shift in UK Policing:

UK Policing.

Andy Rhodes and Ian Hesketh

Covid-19 has also promoted the concept of personalisation. This has happened because the impact of a pandemic is felt differently by every individual. As leaders in health and wellbeing, we have always promoted the concept of the 24/7 person bringing 100% of their uniqueness into the workplace. However, we find this often fails to translate into policy and practice. 'One size fits all' is generally the default position, but we know our ups and downs are never left at the door, so to speak. The Human Resource (HR) and Health and Safety (H&S) functions were required to make decisions about isolation based on a 'whole life' assessment of the individual, and we started to learn more and more about the complicated lives of our people. An officer who, so anxious about the risk of bringing the virus home to a daughter with leukemia, had taken to sleeping in his car on the driveway of his house. So many who were unable to visit elderly relatives or loved ones and sadly unable to grieve normally when they passed.

All of a sudden, the conversation started to change to one that was more compassionate, empathic and less judgemental. Also, it improved the morale of our HR teams who, for the first time, were not simply asked to case-manage the most complex individuals day after day. They were doing what they joined to do, and every force established 24/7 HR teams to advise line managers on the latest guidance and policy changes so that they could, in turn, provide more flexibility for their teams, at their own discretion. We trusted our people at last. In return, their feelings of meaning and purpose increased. The key tenets of well-being were, indeed, improving before our eyes.

SHOW VULNERABILITY

Emotional vulnerability is the willingness and ability to address and articulate emotions, especially those that are uncomfortable or painful. Vulnerability is a core component of authenticity and a key to fostering trust. When a leader acknowledges and embraces one's imperfections, it builds deeper relationships with others and creates a culture of transparency and trust. Ways in which managers can show vulnerability include voicing challenges and mistakes, asking for help, soliciting feedback, standing up for your values and beliefs and sharing personal stories.

This three-step process can help demonstrate vulnerability practically:

1. First **observing** your emotion(s). For example, notice that you are feeling anger, sadness, or anxiety without thinking about it or acting upon it.

2. **Validating** your emotions: Reminding yourself that it is OK to feel whatever emotions you're going through. There is no judgement or self-criticism. Journalling can help.

3. **Opening up**: Once you have acknowledged your emotions and been open and vulnerable to yourself, you can work your way up to being vulnerable with others that you trust and feel safe opening up to.

In the following example, when a senior executive demonstrated vulnerability, it resulted in significant cultural change. This was experienced as a more open and supportive work environment and a social movement that normalised mental health conversations.

GlaxoSmithKline – Sharing my personal experience.

David Gordon – Global Head of Tax

"Supporting wellbeing is an essential part of a leader's role, as a fundamental driver of business performance."

Throughout my career I have always felt like I operate at my best when I am under pressure. When complexity is great, deadlines are short, and expectations are high, that is when I thrive – getting my head down, focusing and delivering, no matter the circumstances.

Having worked in a Big 4 advisory firm, advising private equity clients on M&A deals, and then at GSK, there was no shortage of pressure, no shortage of deadlines and no shortage of working late nights, early mornings and weekends to satisfy demands. But I was resilient – always pushing myself forward and jumping at any opportunity to take on more responsibility and to try something new, no matter what else I had on, or what the impact was on me or my life outside of work – building my reputation as someone who could get gets things done under pressure.

However, eventually the mechanisms to deal with that pressure began to stop working. Life started to change, with additional responsibilities outside of work, like kids and a mortgage, bringing additional pressures, meaning that I could not necessarily work or manage pressure in the same way as before. Things started to become overwhelming, and I started to struggle with anxiety, to the point where it started to become debilitating.

I was struggling to put things into perspective (in both work and my personal life); over-thinking things and becoming indecisive (never a problem for me before); over-preparing for things, with constant very late nights and early mornings, making sure I was over every detail of topics I was discussing with stakeholders; and I started trying to avoid certain situations which could be stressful and bring on my anxiety. I was basically a big ball of anxiety and stress, which led to me being short with my family and generally becoming a person that I didn't want to be.

And then I started having physical symptoms – feeling sick, not eating properly, not sleeping and ultimately culminating in panic attacks, where I was unable to breathe properly.

I clearly knew that I had a problem, but I didn't know where to get help. Luckily, I had people around me (at home and at work) who cared and who could tell that I wasn't myself. At work, a perceptive member of my team left a 'Face the Truth' questionnaire (which allows you to assess how you are looking after yourself) on my desk, and this highlighted to me that I was not looking after myself physically or mentally. And at home, my wife organised for me to see a psychologist, which led to me taking medication and starting Cognitive Behavioural Therapy – both of which helped me to get my anxiety better under control.

Having been through this experience, I wanted to make sure that any of my friends and colleagues who were suffering in silence knew that they could get support if they needed it. In particular, I wanted to end the stigma that surrounds mental health and to create an open culture where it becomes normal to talk about mental health challenges. To do that, I felt strongly that the most impactful thing that I could do was to talk openly about my experiences, to share my story in the hope that this would give others the freedom to do the same. And, when I started to do that, it was a real eye-opener, both in terms of the scale of the issue, with a large number of people reaching out to share their personal stories, and also in terms of the impact that I was having in enabling people to talk openly for the first time.

The task then became to keep it at the forefront of the business agenda. Supporting wellbeing must be seen as an equally important part of a leader's role as driving business performance. We know that engagement links to productivity and employees want to work for organisations that care about their wellbeing, which links to individual and organisational performance.

At GSK, we are doing this through a community of Wellbeing Champions, who are passionate about supporting their colleagues – leading initiatives such as panel events with senior leaders sharing their own experiences; recording podcasts on specific areas of mental health and raising awareness of resources available in the company; setting up listening pods where people can come together in smaller groups to talk and share about issues that are particularly important to them; and organising wellbeing events for their teams, such as exercise challenges.

While we cannot solve people's mental health problems, nor can we cure people or turn our staff into psychologists, what we can do is to help raise the awareness that poor mental health is not uncommon and arm colleagues to have conversations and support and steer people in the right direction so that they get the support they need at the right time.

Supporting line managers to build these core competencies

Roles of the Line Manager

Figure 3.10 The key roles of the line manager in workplace health and wellbeing

It is not uncommon for managers to experience a tension between their desire to support employee wellbeing, and the need to drive company performance. This can result in frustration or insufficient action in relation to supporting their teams. Expectations of their role must be clearly articulated, with access to sufficient support, including training and the space to invest in this fundamental aspect of their role.

In addition to traditional ways of measuring manager performance (i.e., achieving business objectives), assessing performance related to behaviours and their impact on staff wellbeing and experience, will drive a culture that enables employees to thrive. Manager performance criteria can include effectively creating a culture of wellbeing where employees feel supported. This is commonly assessed through company culture and/or manager surveys that include to what extent the manager has supported elements of wellbeing. This helps review the extent to which interventions that aim to enhance manager behaviours have been successful and identify improvement areas, at the individual and organisational levels.

It will be necessary for line managers to have protected time during their workday to carry out this aspect of their role. Manager peer support groups can provide a safe space for managers to debrief, share ideas and learn from each other, through strengthening social networks with others who share similar challenges. Providing managers access to a coach and/or mentor can also support their development in this space, helping them to embed learned behaviours.

UK Policing – Peer-to-Peer support.

Andy Rhodes and Ian Hesketh

We strongly advocate line managers need to have the time to be 'approachable and well informed' and locate them in a safe system. This system includes access to peer groups and clinical services.

ACTIONS

Line manager actions

Self-care:

1. Role model positive wellbeing through daily self-care practices, such as adequate recovery, sleep and physical activity and healthy nutrition.

2. Minimise multitasking and proactively plan your work schedule to maximise effectiveness. Explore opportunities, however short, to pause and be more mindful.

Check-in and build trust:

3. Prioritise EH&W in all discussions, to understand how to support your team and take an individual approach to employee wellbeing, ensuring adequate time and no distractions.
4. Express genuine gratitude in recognition of the contribution of others.
5. Show compassion and share your own vulnerabilities.
6. Check in with your team regularly regarding their wellbeing, within and outside of work. Take a personalised approach to understand the unique needs of individuals. (Questions such as "How are you?", "How are you 'really'?" and "How are you finding your work–life balance?" can be helpful starters.)
7. Consider the possibility of work stress with staff, exploring the range of workplace stressors, using evidence-based frameworks such as the HSE Management Standards, to identify actions to further support their wellbeing.

Self-develop:

8. Undertake available training e.g., self-care/resilience, building better team connection (such as compassion training), developing deeper conversations, spotting the signs of poor mental health and learning how to support individuals.
9. Engage with available support to help embed learned behaviours, e.g. join manager peer networks, seek a coach and/or mentor.

Organisational actions

1. Set clear manager expectations and measure performance.
   Give equal parity to manager behaviours and their technical skills when selecting, promoting, and rewarding managers. Measure desirable behaviours and use this data to drive accountability and inform change.

2. Position EH&W as a core component of leadership development and incorporate EH&W content into leadership development programmes.

3. Offer manager training to build competency in self-care, compassion and giving and receiving feedback, and build manager capability to check in with their staff and have the confidence to spot signs of poor wellbeing, and support staff appropriately. Mandating manager training or setting uptake targets emphasises organisational commitment. To be successful training must be:
   - Easy to access, relevant, engaging, interactive and succinct.
   - Made available to complete during working hours.

4. Provide additional support such as access to coaching, mentorship and manager peer networks, to help leaders to learn and embed desired behaviours and lead their employees in a health-oriented manner.

5. Ensure managers have the bandwidth to engage effectively in this crucial aspect of their role.

REFERENCES

Adler, A.B., Adrian, A.L., Hemphill, M., Scaro, N.H., Sipos, M.L., & Thomas, J.L. (2017). Professional stress and burnout in US military medical personnel deployed to Afghanistan. *Military Medicine, 182* (3–4), 1669–1676.

American Psychological Association. (2014). *The road to resilience.* Washington, DC: American Psychological Association.

Ammar, A., Brach, M., Trabelsi, K., Chtourou, H., Boukhris, O., Masmoudi, L., … & ECLB-COVID19 Consortium. (2020). Effects of COVID-19 home confinement on eating behaviour and physical activity: Results of the ECLB-COVID19 international online survey. *Nutrients, 12*(6), 1583.

Arnetz, B.B., Nevedal, D.C., Lumley, M.A., Backman, L., & Lublin, A. (2009). Trauma resilience training for police: Psychophysiological and performance effects. *Journal of Police and Criminal Psychology, 24*, 1–9.

Arnold, K.A. (2017). Transformational leadership and employee psychological well-being: A review and directions for future research. *Journal of Occupational Health Psychology, 22*(3), 381.

Ayala, E.E., Winseman, J.S., Johnsen, R.D., & Mason, H.R. (2018). US medical students who engage in self-care report less stress and higher quality of life. *BMC Medical Education, 18*(1), 1–9.

Bakker, A.B. (2014). Daily fluctuations in work engagement: An overview and current directions. *European Psychologist, 19*(4), 227–236.

Baldwin Jr., D.C., & Daugherty, S.R. (2004). Sleep deprivation and fatigue in residency training: Results of a national survey of first-and second-year residents. *Sleep*, *27*(2), 217–223.

Baptiste, N.R. (2008). Tightening the link between employee wellbeing at work and performance: A new dimension for HRM. *Management Decision*, *46*(2), 284–309.

Boyatzis, R.E., Smith, M.L., & Blaize, N. (2006). Developing sustainable leaders through coaching and compassion. *Academy of Management Learning & Education*, *5*(1), 8–24.

Brooks, S.K., Dunn, R., Amlôt, R., Rubin, G.J., & Greenberg, N. (2018). A systematic, thematic review of social and occupational factors associated with psychological outcomes in healthcare employees during an infectious disease outbreak. *Journal of Occupational and Environmental Medicine*, *60*(3), 248–257.

Brosschot, J.F., Pieper, S., & Thayer, J.F. (2005). Expanding stress theory: Prolonged activation and perseverative cognition. *Psychoneuroendocrinology*, *30*, 1043–1049.

Bryan, M., & Nandi, A. (2015). Working hours, work identity and subjective wellbeing (No. 2015–21). *ISER Working Paper Series*.

Buckley, J.P., Mellor, D.D., Morris, M., & Joseph, F. (2014). Standing-based office work shows encouraging signs of attenuating post-prandial glycaemic excursion. *Occupational and Environmental Medicine*, *71*(2), 109–111.

Cancelliere, C., Cassidy, J.D., Ammendolia, C., & Côté, P. (2011). Are workplace health promotion programs effective at improving presenteeism in workers? A systematic review and best evidence synthesis of the literature. *BMC Public Health*, *11*(1), 1–11.

Chu, L.C. (2016). Mediating positive moods: The impact of experiencing compassion at work. *Journal of Nursing Management*, *24*(1), 59–69.

Conner, T.S., Brookie, K.L., Richardson, A.C., & Polak, M.A.. (2015). On carrots and curiosity: Eating fruit and vegetables is associated with greater flourishing in daily life. *British Journal of Health Psychology*, *20*(2), 413–427.

Cortini, M., Converso, D., Galanti, T., Fiore, T., Di Domenico, A., & Fantinelli, S. (2019). Gratitude at work works! A mix-method study on different dimensions of gratitude, job satisfaction, and job performance. *Sustainability*, *11*, 3902.

Coulson, J.C., McKenna, J., & Field, M. (2008). Exercising at work and self-reported work performance. *International Journal of Workplace Health Management*, *1*(3), 176–197.

Crews, D., & Russ, M. (2012). The impact of multitasking on human and organizational efficiency. *Leadership & Organizational Management Journal*, *2012*(3).

Dutton, J., Workman, K., & Hardin, A. (2014). Compassion at work. *Annual Review of Organizational Psychology and Organizational Behavior*, 1, 277–304.

Eldor, L. (2017). Public service sector: The compassionate workplace – The effect of compassion and stress on employee engagement, burnout, and performance. *Journal of Public Administration Research and Theory, 2017*, 1–18.

Fletcher, D. & Sarkar, M. (2013). Psychological resilience. *European Psychologist, 18*, 12–23.

Franke, F., Felfe, J., & Pundt, A. (2014). The impact of health-oriented leadership on follower health: Development and test of a new instrument measuring health-promoting leadership. *German Journal of Human Resource Management, 28*(1/2), 139–161.

Galabova, L., & McKie, L. (2013). The five fingers of my hand: Human capital and well-being in SMEs. *Personnel Review, 42*(6), 662–683.

Gilbert, P., McEwan, K., Matos, M., & Rivis, A. (2011). Fear of compassion: Development of three self-report measures. *Journal of Psychology and Psychotherapy, 84*, 239–255.

Gorgievski, M.J., & Hobfoll, S.E. 2008. Work can burn us out or fire us up: Conservation of resources in burnout and engagement. In J.R.B. Halbesleben (Ed.), *Handbook of stress and burnout in health care*, pp. 7–22. Hauppauge, NY: Nova Science.

Grant, A.M., Dutton, J.E., & Rosso, B.D. (2008). Giving commitment: Employee support programs and the prosocial sensemaking process. *Academy of Management Journal, 51*, 898–918.

Guarana, C., & Barnes, C. (2017). Lack of sleep and the development of leader-follower relationships over time. *Organizational Behavior and Human Decision Processes, 141*, 57–73.

Halbesleben, J.R., & Rathert, C. (2008). Linking physician burnout and patient outcomes: Exploring the dyadic relationship between physicians and patients. *Health Care Management Review, 33*(1), 29–39.

Hallal, P.C., Andersen, L.B., Bull, F.C., Guthold, R., Haskell, W., Ekelund, U., & Lancet Physical Activity Series Working Group. (2012). Global physical activity levels: Surveillance progress, pitfalls, and prospects. *The Lancet, 380*, 247–257.

Halliwell, E. (2010). *Mindfulness-Report 2010*. UK: Mental Health Foundation.

Hansen, C.J., Stevens, L.C., & Coast, J.R. (2001). Exercise duration and mood state: How much is enough to feel better? *Health Psychology, 20*(4), 267.

Health and Safety Executive. (n.d.-a). Work-related stress and how to manage it. Retrieved November 25, from https://www.hse.gov.uk/stress/overview.htm

Health and Safety Executive. (n.d.-b). What are the management standards? Retrieved November 25, from https://www.hse.gov.uk/stress/standards/

Howe, A., Smajdor, A., & Stöckl, A. (2012). Towards an understanding of resilience and its relevance to medical training. *Medical Education, 46*(4), 349–356.

Huo, M.-L., Boxall, P., & Cheung, G.W. (2022). Lean production, work intensification and employee wellbeing: Can line-manager support make a difference? *Economic and Industrial Democracy, 43*(1), 198–220.

Jensen, C.G., Lansner, J., Petersen, A., Vangkilde, S.A., Ringkøbing, S.P., Frokjaer, V.G., … & Hasselbalch, S.G. (2015). Open and Calm–A randomized controlled trial evaluating a public stress reduction program in Denmark. *BMC Public Health*, *15*, 1–13.

Kahn, W.A. (1990). Psychological conditions of personal engagement and disengagement at work. *The Academy of Management Journal*, *33*(4), 692–724.

Kaluza, A.J., Weber, F., van Dick, R., Junker, N.M. (2021). When and how health-oriented leadership relates to employee well-being—The role of expectations, self-care, and LMX. *Journal of Applied Social Psychology*, *51*, 404–424.

Kark, R., & Carmeli, A. (2009). Alive and creating: The mediating role of vitality and aliveness in the relationship between psychological safety and creative work involvement. *Journal of Organizational Behavior*, *30*(6), 785–804.

Kent de Grey, R.G., Uchino, B.N., Trettevik, R., et al. (2018). Social support and sleep: A meta-analysis. *Health Psychology*, *37*, 787–798.

Kotera, Y., Richardson, M., & Sheffield, D. (2020). Effects of Shinrin-Yoku (forest bathing) and nature therapy on mental health: A systematic review and meta-analysis. *International Journal of Mental Health and Addiction*, *63*.

Lamb, D., et al. (2021). The psychosocial impact of COVID-19 pandemic on 4,378 UK healthcare workers and ancillary staff: Initial baseline data from a cohort study collected during the first wave of the pandemic. *Occupational and Environmental Medicine*, *78*(11), 801–808.

Lester, P., Taylor, L., Hawkins, S., & Landry, L. (2015). Current directions in military health-care provider resilience. *Current Psychiatry Reports*, *17*(6), 1–7.

MacLean, K.A., Ferrer, E., Aichele, S.R., Bridwell, D.A., Zanesco, A.P., Jacobs, T.L., … & Saron, C.D. (2010). Intensive meditation training improves perceptual discrimination and sustained attention. *Psychological Science*, *21*(6), 829–839.

Madore, K.P., & Wagner, A.D., (2019). Multicosts of multitasking. In *Cerebrum: The Dana forum on brain science*. Dana Foundation.

Myers, D.G. (2003). Close relationships and quality of life. In D. Kahneman, E. Diener, N. Schwarz (Eds.), *Well-Being: The foundations of hedonic psychology* (pp. 374–391). New York: Russell Sage Foundation Publications.

McGarrigle, T., & Walsh, C.A. (2011). Mindfulness, self-care, and wellness in social work: Effects of contemplative training. *Journal of Religion & Spirituality in Social Work: Social Thought*, *30*(3), 212–233.

Monroe, C., Loresto, F., Horton-Deutsch, S., Kleiner, C., Eron, K., Varney, R., & Grimm, S. (2021). The value of intentional self-care practices: The effects of mindfulness on improving job satisfaction, teamwork, and workplace environments. *Archives of Psychiatric Nursing*, *35*(2), 189–194.

Nordin, M., Knutsson, A., & Sundbom, E. (2008). Is disturbed sleep a mediator in the association between social support and myocardial infarction? *Journal of Health Psychology*, *13*, 55–64.

Nyberg, A., Alfredsson, L., Theorell, T., et al. (2009). Managerial leadership and ischaemic heart disease among employees: The Swedish WOLF study. *Occupational and Environmental Medicine, 66,* 51–55.

Oppezzo, M., & Schwartz, D.L. (2014). Give your ideas some legs: The positive effect of walking on creative thinking. *Journal of Experimental Psychology: Learning, Memory, and Cognition, 40*(4), 1142.

Ostafin, B.D., & Kassman, K.T. (2012). Stepping out of history: Mindfulness improves insight problem solving. *Consciousness and Cognition, 21*(2), 1031–1036.

Paakkanen, M., Martela, F., Hakanen, J., Uusitalo, L., & Pessi, A. (2021). Awakening compassion in managers – A new emotional skills intervention to improve managerial compassion. *Journal of Business and Psychology, 36,* 1095–1108.

Patterson, R., McNamara, E., Tainio, M., de Sá, T.H., Smith, A.D., Sharp, S.J., … Wijndaele, K. (2018). Sedentary behaviour and risk of all-cause, cardiovascular and cancer mortality, and incident type 2 diabetes: A systematic review and dose response meta-analysis. *European Journal of Epidemiology, 33,* 811–829.

Petrie, K., Gayed, A., Bryan, B.T., Deady, M., Madan, I., Savic, A., et al. (2018). The importance of manager support for the mental health and well-being of ambulance personnel. *PLoS ONE, 13*(5), e0197802.

Pipe, T.B., Buchda, V.L., Launder, S., Hudak, B., Hulvey, L., Karns, K.E., & Pendergast, D. (2012). Building personal and professional resources of resilience and agility in the healthcare workplace. *Stress and Health, 28*(1), 11–22.

Poldrack, R.A., & Foerde, K. (2007). Category learning and the memory systems debate. *Neuroscience & Biobehavioral Reviews, 32,* 197–205.

Polizzi, C., Lynn, S.J., & Perry, A. (2020). Stress and coping in the time of COVID-19: Pathways to resilience and recovery. *Clinical Neuropsychiatry, 17,* 59–62.

Roberts, R., Wong, A., Jenkins, S., Neher, A., Sutton, C., O'Meara, P., … & Dwivedi, A. (2021). Mental health and well-being impacts of COVID-19 on rural paramedics, police, community nurses and child protection workers. *Australian Journal of Rural Health, 29*(5), 753–767.

Rodriguez-Vega, B., Palao, Á., Muñoz-Sanjose, A., Torrijos, M., Aguirre, P., Fernández, A., … & Bayón, C. (2020). Implementation of a mindfulness-based crisis intervention for frontline healthcare workers during the COVID-19 outbreak in a public general hospital in Madrid, Spain. *Frontiers in Psychiatry,* 1170.

Rook, J.W., & Zijlstra, F.R.H. (2006). The contribution of various types of activities to recovery. *European Journal of Work and Organizational Psychology, 15*(2), 218–240.

Scarlet, J., Altmeyer, N., Knier, S., & Harpin, E. (2017). The effects of compassion cultivation training (CCT) on health-care workers. *Clinical Psychologist, 21,* 116–124.

Schliemann, D., & Woodside, J. (2019). The effectiveness of dietary workplace interventions: A systematic review of systematic reviews. *Public Health Nutrition, 22*(5), 942–955. doi:10.1017/S1368980018003750.

Shanafelt, T.D., Makowski, M.S., Wang, H., Bohman, B., Leonard, M., Harrington, R.A., Minor, L., & Trockel, M. (2020). Association of burnout, professional fulfillment, and self-care practices of physician leaders with their independently rated leadership effectiveness. *JAMA Network Open, 3*(6), 207961.

Shatté, A., Perlman, A., Smith, B., & Lynch, W.D. (2017). The positive effect of resilience on stress and business outcomes in difficult work environments. *Journal of Occupational and Environmental Medicine, 59*(2), 135.

Sonnentag, S. (2003). Recovery, work engagement, and proactive behavior: A new look at the interface between non-work and work. *Journal of Applied Psychology, 88*(3), 518–528.

Stathopoulou, G., Powers, M.B., Berry, A.C., Smits, J.A., & Otto, M.W. (2006). Exercise interventions for mental health: A quantitative and qualitative review. *Clinical Psychology: Science and Practice, 13*(2), 179.

Steidle, A., Gonzalez-Morales, M., Hoppe, A., Michel, A., & O'Shea, D. (2017). Energizing respites from work: A randomized controlled study on respite interventions. *European Journal of Work and Organizational Psychology, 26*(5), 650–662.

Suija-Markova, I., Briede, L., Gaile-Sarkane, E., & Ozolina-Ozola, I. (2020). Multitasking in knowledge intensive business services. *Emerging Science Journal, 4*(4), 305–318.

Thompson, C.A., & Prottas, D.J. (2006). Relationships among organizational family support, job autonomy, perceived control, and employee well-being. *Journal of Occupational Health Psychology, 11*(2), 100–118.

Tugade, M.M., & Fredrickson, B.L. (2004). Resilient individuals use positive emotions to bounce back from negative emotional experiences. *Journal of Personality and Social Psychology, 86*(2), 320–333.

Wald, J., Taylor, S., Asmundson, G.J., Jang, K.L., & Stapleton, J. (2006). *Literature review of concepts: Psychological resiliency.* Vancouver, Canada: British Columbia University.

Winbush, N.Y., Gross, C.R., & Kreitzer, M.J. (2007). The effects of mindfulness-based stress reduction on sleep disturbance: A systematic review. *Explore, 3*(6), 585–591.

Winwood, P.C., Colon, R., & McEwen, K. (2013). A practical measure of workplace resilience. *Journal of Occupational and Environmental Medicine, 55*(10), 1205–1212.

West, M.A., & Anderson, N.R. (1996). Innovation in top management teams. *Journal of Applied Psychology, 81*(6), 680–693.

Wood, A.M., Maltby, J., Gillett, R., Linley, P.A., & Joseph, S. (2008). The role of gratitude in the development of social support, stress, and depression: Two longitudinal studies. *Journal of Research in Personality, 42*(4), 854–871.

World Health Organization. (2019). Burn-out an "occupational phenomenon": International Classification of Diseases. Retrieved November 25, from https://www.who.int/news/item/28-05-2019-burn-out-an-occupational-phenomenon-international-classification-of-diseases

Wright, L., Steptoe, A., & Fancourt, D. (2021). Are adversities and worries during the COVID-19 pandemic related to sleep quality? Longitudinal analyses of 46,000 UK adults. *PLoS ONE, 16*(3), e0248919.

Wu, A.W., Connors, C., & Everly, G.S. Jr. (2020). COVID-19: Peer support and crisis communication strategies to promote institutional resilience. *Annals of Internal Medicine. 172*(12), 822–823.

Xue, Z., Lin, L., Zhang, S., Gong, J., Liu, J., & Lu, J. (2020). Sleep problems and medical isolation during the SARS-CoV-2 outbreak. *Sleep Medicine, 70,* 112.

Yildirim, M., & Alanazi, Z.S. (2018). Gratitude and life satisfaction: Mediating role of perceived stress. *International Journal of Psychological Studies, 10*(3), 21–28.

Zhang, Y., Fang, Y., Wei, K.K., & Chen, H. (2010). Exploring the role of psychological safety in promoting the intention to continue sharing knowledge in virtual communities. *International Journal of Information Management, 30*(5), 425–436.

Zheng, Z., Gangaram, P., Xie, H., Chua, S., Ong, S.B.C., & Koh, S.E. (2017). Job satisfaction and resilience in psychiatric nurses: A study at the Institute of Mental Health, Singapore. *International Journal of Mental Health Nursing, 26*(6), 612–619.

4

WELLBEING IN THE CONTEXT OF DIVERSITY, EQUITY AND INCLUSION

Key messages

1. To fully maximise wellbeing, engagement, and productivity, organisations must advance their Diversity, Equity and Inclusion (DEI) agenda.

2. Health and wellbeing strategies and resources must be equitable, and sufficiently inclusive, to meet the needs of a diverse workforce.

3. Line managers play a significant role in ensuring diversity, equity and inclusion. By listening to employee concerns, prioritising and promoting self-care among employee groups to build personal resilience and creating support networks, managers can enable employees to maximise their physical and mental health.

4. It is not uncommon for leaders and managers to assume that the chances of developing poor mental and physical health are equal among all employees, who will therefore need a similar approach. The pandemic however highlighted vulnerabilities of certain groups of employees and those in certain professions and roles. For instance, employees from an ethnic minority background, low-income groups, females, those in the younger age bracket and those with pre-existing mental health conditions were at particularly high risk of poor mental and/or physical health. Those working in the frontline at the height of the pandemic were at greatest risk of physical and mental ill health, although essential workers outside of health or social care were also significantly impacted.

DOI: 10.4324/9781003124979-4

5. Manager training must include raising awareness of the differing wellbeing needs of diverse employees and groups that may be at a higher risk of poor health and wellbeing, who require a tailored and targeted approach.
6. Leaders should sponsor and encourage the creation of employee resource groups (ERGs) to provide social support and advocacy for specific employee groups. These groups are a platform to promote employee wellbeing.
7. Longstanding stigma around mental ill health prevents many accessing timely support. Stigma is more pronounced within certain groups and cultures, such as the male population and minority ethic groups.
8. Stigma associated with poor mental ill health prevents staff, across all levels of the organisation, that are experiencing mental health challenges, from accessing the right support at the right time.
9. Efforts focussed on normalising feelings of distress, and encouraging staff to express how they feel will give employees the confidence to open up about how they feel. This should involve organisational-, leader-, team- and employee-level actions.
10. The pandemic shone a light on the extent of caring responsibilities employees undertook, the challenges they faced and how they can be supported. Carers make up a significant proportion of the workforce and must have the right support so that they can be at their best.

INTRODUCTION

There are several factors that determine our health and wellbeing and some of us are more vulnerable to poorer wellbeing than others. Knowing the groups that are a greater risk allows us to be more sensitive and adopt a targeted and tailored approach to meet their needs.

GROUPS AT GREATER RISK OF POOR WELLBEING

By role

The pandemic emphasised the unique physical and mental risks that come with different types of roles and the opportunities to address these. Employees in certain occupations faced greater challenges during the pandemic. They included employees within healthcare, police, and non-healthcare essential workers.

The UK government defined a 'key worker' during the coronavirus (Covid-19) pandemic as a public sector or private sector employee who was considered to provide an 'essential service'. They were also known as 'essential workers'. Their role could not be done outside their usual place of work. In 2019, 10.6 million of those employed in the UK (33% of the total workforce) were in key worker occupations and industries. The largest group of those employed in key worker occupations (31%) worked in health and social care (McSweeney, 2020).

The CIPD's Good Work Index surveyed more than 5000 UK workers across different sectors and occupations about key aspects of their work and employment. The 2021 report showed that *key workers* reported less positive mental and physical health compared to non-key workers (Norris-Green and Gifford, 2021). Unsurprisingly, frontline employees who provided essential services, such as healthcare, grocery stores, pharmacies and long-term care homes, faced increasing health risks in terms of infection, stress and mental illness (Sim, 2020).

Key workers in health and social care

Many frontline health and social care professionals expressed gratitude for being able to continue working and described a sense of increased purpose and reward for being able to contribute during the pandemic (Aughterson et al., 2021). Positive outcomes included greater solidarity between colleagues and high levels of morale amongst UK hospital-based healthcare workers during Covid-19 (Vindrola-Padros et al., 2020). These are in keeping with previous pandemics such as Severe Acute Respiratory Syndrome (SARS) and Middle East Respiratory Syndrome (MERS), where beneficial outcomes included a more positive outlook towards work, growth under pressure, greater camaraderie with colleagues and a strong sense of professional responsibility and personal development (Lee et al., 2005). While these were some of the positive experiences, there were many challenges, particularly in relation to mental health.

Challenges experienced by healthcare workers included a greater risk of developing Covid-19, which had implications for their mental health. In one study, the increase in overall self-reported stress was significantly associated with the lack of workplace health and safety policy in place, inadequate comprehensiveness, lack of timeliness, and lack of protective equipment supply (Wong et al., 2020).

Previous research exploring the psychological impact on health and social care professionals during epidemics such as SARS and MERS), also highlighted the adverse psychological effects on healthcare workers (Wu et al., 2009) during epidemics (McAlonan et al., 2007). To add to this, we now know that the Coronavirus Disease 2019 (Covid-19) pandemic resulted in an overall surge in new cases of depression and anxiety and an exacerbation of existing mental health issues, with a particular emotional and physical toll on healthcare workers (Lai et al., 2020).

The prevalence of psychological ill health, such as anxiety, among healthcare workers during the pandemic was significantly higher than among the general population (Liu et al., 2020) with frontline workers most impacted (Gilleen et al., 2021). Stressors or root causes included limited resources, longer shifts, disruptions to sleep and to work–life balance, and occupational hazards associated with exposure to Covid-19, which contributed to physical and mental fatigue, stress and anxiety, and burnout (Adam & Walls, 2020). Among healthcare workers, nurses were reported to experience the highest levels of anxiety (Luo et al., 2020) likely due to working on the frontline. In fact, a case-control study recruiting 1173 frontline and 1173 age- and sex-matched non-frontline medical workers during the Covid-19 outbreak found that the rate of mental health problems, such as anxiety, depression, and insomnia, was significantly increased in frontline medical workers, compared with non-frontline medical workers (Cai et al., 2020). In particular, frontline medical workers directly dealing with patients confirmed or suspected of having Covid-19 had higher levels of various mental health problems than non-frontline medical workers (Cai et al., 2020). Of interest, both groups had comparable low rates of help-seeking behaviours and treatment for their mental problems, highlighting the need to promote the availability and uptake of resources available and normalise conversations around mental health. This is vital to allow us to reduce the stigma that continues to exist. Managers can play a pivotal role in this.

Dr Danielle Lamb, a co-investigator on a study on NHS workers during the Pandemic, highlights the scale of mental health challenges amongst NHS workers and the opportunity for managers to provide support to their staff:

NHS: The Mental Health and Wellbeing of UK NHS workers.

Dr Danielle Lamb, Senior Research Fellow, University College London.

The NHS CHECK study is a longitudinal cohort study of the mental health and wellbeing of UK NHS workers that began during the Covid-19 pandemic (Lamb et al., 2021a). The study primarily consists of online surveys completed in four phases (at baseline from April 2020, and then 6 months, 12 months, and 32 months after baseline), but includes several sub-studies (a diagnostic interview study, qualitative interview studies, and a randomised controlled trial of a smartphone wellbeing app). Staff from 18 NHS Trusts across England were recruited, including acute and mental health Trusts. The baseline survey included questions about: 1) impact of Covid-19 (e.g. on family, income, health, positive and negative changes in personal life or work), 2) work experiences (leadership and teamwork, sickness absence, unsafe clinical practices, preparedness), 3) usefulness of staff support programmes, 4) caring responsibilities outside of work, 5) confidence in institutions to handle the Covid-19 pandemic. The study represents a large sample size (N > 23,000) with similar demographic characteristics to the overall NHS workforce in terms of age and sex, though proportionally fewer participants from minoritised racial and ethnic groups. Preliminary data showed high levels of distress and symptoms associated with common mental disorders, substantially high levels of probable common mental disorders (59%) and probable post-traumatic stress disorder (PTSD) (30%) (Lamb et al., 2021b). With the notable exception of PTSD, the results are comparable to findings from previous epidemics; however, this may be a result of differing PTSD measures and cut-off scores between the studies. In line with other studies, compared with general population data which used the same measure and cut-off score, there was a much higher prevalence of symptoms of mental disorders in healthcare workers. Subsequent analyses of gold standard psychiatric diagnostic interviews found that the screening measures used in the online surveys are likely to overestimate the prevalence of mental disorders, with more accurate estimated population prevalence of generalised anxiety disorder and depression of 22%, and of PTSD of 8% (Scott et al., 2023). While much lower than the numbers found by large-scale surveys, these still show concerning levels of diagnosable mental disorders in the healthcare workforce. Similarly, an analysis of data regarding suicidal thoughts and behaviours in this cohort also found concerning evidence (Padmanathan et al., 2023). At baseline and 6 months later, 11% and 9% (respectively) of participants reported recent suicidal thoughts, 2% reported a recent suicide attempt, and 3% reported recent self-harm. As these data were longitudinal, it was possible to find out that, of those who at baseline reported no history of ever attempting suicide, 4% reported a suicide attempt 6 months later. More in-depth analysis and qualitative research is needed to unpick the reasons for these worrying findings, but one factor that seems to be implicated in a number of poor mental health outcomes is moral injury. Originating in military research, the concept of moral injury refers to the psychological harm caused by either witnessing or participating in actions that transgress one's moral beliefs. Data from the baseline survey show that 28% of participants reported experiencing potentially morally injurious events, and that those people were statistically significantly more likely to also experience symptoms of PTSD, anxiety, depression, and burnout (Williamson et al., 2023). Qualitative work on this issue has found that healthcare workers feel they have been betrayed by government and NHS leaders, and have been put in positions where they are unable to provide the appropriate quality of care to patients. The impacts of these morally injurious experiences were described as increased anxiety and depression, and sleep disturbance, with most participants believing that organisational change was necessary to reduce or prevent exposure to such experiences, and support the resolution of moral distress (Hegarty et al., 2022). Additional qualitative interviews with healthcare workers about their experiences of health and wellbeing support services also found that systemic issues such as workload and understaffing (and the related socio-political contexts of austerity and Brexit) played a large role in whether participants were able to access support (Clarkson et al., 2023). Things that enabled use of support services were visible, caring leadership at all levels (CEO to line managers), peer support, easily accessible services, and clear communication about support offers.

Perceptions of Support

Nearly half of staff (49%) felt supported by managers, 61% felt supported by colleagues, 76% felt supported by family.

Over 11% of staff reported feeling not at all supported by supervisors or line managers.

Most used support services

66%
STAFF DISCOUNTS
This was also seen as the most helpful service

40%
ONLINE RESOURCES
not specific to the NHS, recommended by colleagues, family, or friends

35%
FREE WELLBEING APPS

Least used support services

5%
BEREAVEMENT SUPPORT LINE

6%
STAFF SUPPORT TEXT LINE

7%
STAFF SUPPORT PHONE LINE

How your participation is helping

Already our research is making an impact. It has been included in government reports and shared widely with other researchers working in healthcare.

To find out more visit nhscheck.org/how-its-helping

Figure 4.1 NHS CHECK study findings on perceptions and sources of support for mental health and wellbeing

There is a real opportunity to help managers to support their teams through line manager training focussed on self-care, checking in and creating psychological safety. (Chapter 3 expands on these areas).

A UK qualitative study interviewing 25 participants from a range of frontline professions in health and social care in the UK during the Covid-19 pandemic discovered three factors that helped alleviate distress and contribute to the resilience of health and social care professionals during the pandemic: 'support structures' (consisting of 'team unity', 'leadership' and 'social support'), 'resilience' (consisting of 'proactive coping', 'accepting uncertainty' and 'increased sense of purpose and reward') and 'personal growth' (consisting of 'slowing down', 'increased reflection' and 'improved relationships') (Aughterson et al., 2021). Focussed support around these areas remains as relevant today for employees both within and outside health and social care and can be a useful guide for all managers. This study highlights that the responsibility lies not only with the individual but also with line managers to support these three areas.

In line with these findings, enhancing social support and connection have been shown to make a big difference to the resilience and wellbeing of healthcare workers, and perceived social support has been found to mediate the relationship between nurses' workplace stress and their burnout (Liu, & Aungsuroch, 2019). A study on 325 nurses in the Philippines found that increased levels of personal resilience, organisational support and social support in nurses were associated with decreased levels of anxiety related to Covid-19 (Labrague & de Los Santos, 2020) and a recent systematic review of quantitative studies examining the impact of Covid-19 on healthcare workers found that coping was enhanced by good social support (Labrague, 2021).

Concerns about the mental health and wellbeing of health and social care professionals in the UK were already growing prior to the Covid-19 pandemic, with 'professional burnout' recognised as a particular challenge (Imo, 2017). The pandemic emphasised the need to prioritise mental wellbeing support to healthcare and social care workers.

Non-healthcare key workers

Policing

Police officers were confronted with various novel challenges during the Covid-19 pandemic. An online survey of 2567 police officers (77% male) from Austria, Germany, Switzerland, the Netherlands, and Spain early 2020 investigated officers' strain over a three-month-period after lockdown (Frenkel et al., 2021). Stressor appraisal (reinterpreting a negative event in a positive manner and trying to find opportunities for learning and growth), emotion regulation (the ability to exert control over one's own emotional state), and preparedness were among the factors that significantly predicted strain. The main stressors were risk of infection and deficient communication. Emotion regulation strategies such as reappraisal have been shown to decrease negative affect (the experience of feeling or emotion) and increase positive affect, while maladaptive strategies (e.g., suppression) increase negative affect and decrease positive affect (Brans et al., 2013).

A deeper dive on preparedness amongst European police officers found that feeling prepared for the pandemic through training on specific police skills significantly reduced strain and aided coping (Frenkel et al., 2021). Specifically, situational response training that included stress regulation through using helpful adaptive emotion regulation such as reflection, reappraisal, social sharing and distraction, reduced officers' strain during the pandemic.

To mitigate against the impact of stressful work demands, organisations may consider proactively offering foundation training on stress regulation and resilience, to build employees skills in managing stress early, to prevent longer-term effects (see 'self-care' section in Chapter 3.

Low-income employee groups

In contrast to the early stages of the pandemic, where greatest impact on wellbeing was experienced amongst health and social care workers, a large UK study on over 20,000 adults conducted over 12 months that differentiated category of key worker, found that it was only key workers carrying out *'essential services'* such as utility, food chain, and transport that had *consistently* higher levels of depressive and anxiety symptoms than non-key workers across the entire 12-month study period (Paul et al., 2021). Additionally, an Australian study identified greater stress and worse quality of life amongst key workers outside the healthcare sector versus healthcare workers and the general population (Toh et al., 2021). The authors hypothesised that this was due to receiving less recognition for their efforts from their employers or the public and being disproportionally more likely to have lower levels of educational attainment, to be in more routine occupational roles, and to experience financial hardship than other categories of key workers and the general population (Marmot et al., 2008). Low-income workers are more likely to have jobs deemed as essential with no options for flexibility of working from home, and workplace exposures posing significant risks. Organisations must consider offering financial wellbeing support and offering more flexibility to their workers who cannot conduct their duties outside their usual place of work, such as greater choice on work scheduling, and reward and recognise them adequately.

Organisations may also benefit from financially supporting employees to access medical care, as in the following example from Transport for London, with gains for the individual and the organisation.

TfL medical assistance programme.

Dr Samantha Phillips. Head of Health and Wellbeing. Transport for London.

We have a small budget available to provide investigations or treatment for employees where it will enable them to return to work and where the waiting time for NHS treatment would lead to prolonged absence. There are a number of eligibility criteria and requests are considered by a multidisciplinary clinical committee to ensure that the criteria are applied consistently. This has been particularly useful in helping to alleviate long term absence due to prolonged NHS waiting times as a result of the pandemic.

Ethnic minority groups

Targeting employee groups that are at the greatest risk of poor wellbeing can maximise engagement and have the greatest impact on reducing health risks and maximising engagement and productivity. The first step is to use your evidence base to identify which health conditions are worth preventing or managing better (i.e. those that enhance individual health and wellbeing, which will ultimately have positive business benefits). The next step is to identify those 'at risk' to help target health promotion efforts. Two examples that follow illustrate this.

John Lewis – Screening for high-risk groups – BAME.

Dr Nick Davison.

Diabetes Screening

During the first year of the Covid-19 pandemic, 2020, the *Disparities in the risks and outcomes of Covid-19* report was published by Public Health England. This highlighted that people from Black and Asian ethnic groups were most likely to be diagnosed with Covid-19 and experienced the highest death rates, and this was the opposite of previous experience.

Furthermore, diabetes was cited on 21% of death certificates where Covid-19 was also mentioned, indicating a higher risk of death from the disease among patients with diabetes. However, the impact of diabetes and Covid-19 was significantly higher in Black patients at a 45% death rate and in Asian patients at a 43% death rate.

In response, John Lewis Partnership initiated a diabetes screening programme in London to establish a baseline of the risks for its Partners (employees), which began in October 2020. The screening programme was deliberately promoted to the Partnership's Black and Asian Partners, but was available to all ethnic groups.

The second UK lockdown placed a premature halt to the screening but 287 Partners were engaged in being weighed, BMI calculated, waist measurement, blood pressure and urine sample taken and the Diabetes UK Risk Assessment completed. The sample size has a 90% confidence rating and a 5% margin of error.

The age profile of those completing the screening were 54% female and 46% male. In terms of age, 21% Under 30 yrs old, 35% 30–50 yrs old and 44% aged 50 years or more.

The ethnicity profile was 25% Asian, 20% Black, 2% Chinese, 11% Mixed Race, 40% White.

The results from the screening found that 13% of those screened were at High Risk of diabetes with 32% at Moderate Risk, 39% at Increased Risk and 16% at Low Risk.

There were variations by ethnicity, with Asian employees representing 25% of those screened but 32% of those at High Risk. Female Asian employees were the single largest cohort in the High-Risk category.

Black Partners represented 20% of those screened but 30% of those at High Risk.

By contrast, White Partners recorded the lowest proportions at High Risk and the highest at Low Risk.

Whilst the screening programme was cut short by Covid-19 restrictions the results demonstrated the significant risk that diabetes poses to the working population, especially when considered in the context of the pandemic. The results have been used to promote healthier lifestyle choices internally and led to the delivery of an 'Eat Well, Live Well' campaign which is now run annually.

UK Policing. Supporting high risk groups.

Andy Rhodes and Dr Ian Hesketh.

High-risk groups, such as those requiring shielding, BAME, and those in certain higher-risk roles, were provided 1-to-1 risk assessments. The NPWS presented options for agreement at the national level, after close consultation with the Department of Health and Social Care (DHSC) and Public Health England (which now is largely the UK Health Security Agency).

We also established a national group to rapidly develop policy as and when evidence came out, regarding BAME risk for example. Closely working with staff networks and unions we collaborated to ensure we can respond fast to assuage fears and build trust.

Female gender and younger adults

A systematic review synthesising literature on the effects of the Covid-19 pandemic on psychological outcomes of the general population found that relatively high rates of symptoms of anxiety, depression, post-traumatic stress disorder, psychological distress and stress were reported in the general population during the Covid-19 pandemic in a range of countries: China, Spain, Italy, Iran, the US, Turkey, Nepal and Denmark (Xiong et al., 2020). Risk factors associated with distress included female gender and younger age group (≤40 years).

A UK community study of over 3000 people (over 18 years old) on reported mental health, during the first 4–6 weeks of social distancing measures being introduced, found increased psychological morbidity in the form of depression, stress and anxiety particularly in younger people, women and in individuals who identified as being in recognised Covid-19 risk groups (Jia et al., 2020). A study based on an online survey of 1,982 adult residents of the United Kingdom of Great Britain and Northern Ireland (UK) (Fujiwara et al., 2020), found that in addition to women and key workers, higher levels of daily anxiety was worse for ethnic minority groups. An online survey of 1005 people four weeks following lockdown in Austria (Pieh et al., 2020) found that the pandemic and lockdown particularly impacted younger adults (<35 years), women and low-income groups.

Loneliness has been a major concern as a result of the pandemic and is a big risk factor for poor mental wellbeing. To assess the impact of the pandemic and associated lockdowns during the initial lockdown phase (March–July 2020), data on 205,084 individuals from seven studies from Denmark, France, and the Netherlands, found that loneliness and anxiety were amongst the main outcomes (Varga et al., 2021). Younger individuals and individuals with a history of mental illness expressed the highest levels of loneliness. Similar groups to those at higher risk in the general population have been seen to struggle in the workplace. Remote workers who were single and childless were identified as being at high risk of feelings of social exclusion and loneliness (Achor et al., 2018).

Preliminary findings from the NHS CHECK study on clinical and non-clinical staff of London-based NHS trusts (UK), including acute and mental health trusts found women, younger staff, and nurses tended to have poorer mental health outcomes than other staff.

UK Office of National Statistics (ONS) data in early 2021 found that approximately 1 in 5 (21%) UK adults experienced some form of depression in early 2021, more than double the rate observed before the coronavirus pandemic (10%) (Williams et al., 2021). Within this figure, younger adults and women were more likely to experience some form of depression. Additionally, as much as 28% of adults living in the most deprived areas of England experienced depressive symptoms, compared with 17% adults in the least deprived areas.

Hybrid working women experienced a significant impact on their wellbeing (see Chapter 5 on women and hybrid working).

Ways in which organisations support their female and younger staff included specific career development programmes, coaching, mentorship programmes and creating ERGs for these groups. Managers may wish to check in more frequently with these groups to find ways to enhance their wellbeing, including encouraging social connections.

Carers

Caregivers are an often-forgotten employee group, yet are navigating significantly demanding responsibilities. Family caregivers of cancer patients have been shown to report a number of physical health problems, such as fatigue and sleep disruption (Stenberg et al., 2010). A six-year longitudinal study of caregivers of women with ovarian cancer in Australia found that 56% of the 101 caregivers studied reported one or more negative changes in terms of their physical health since becoming a caregiver, such as gaining weight or reducing their amount of physical exercise (Beesley et al., 2011). Caregivers can feel stressed about meeting work demands which impacts upon their ability to work effectively (Swanberg, 2006) missing time from work to provide informal care and being less able to concentrate on the job. In a study of individuals who cared for older adults, caregiving was associated with an overall loss of just over 20% in workplace productivity through a combination of both greater absenteeism and presenteeism (Giovannetti et al., 2009). The 2022 UK CIPD Wellbeing at Work survey report encouragingly found that a substantial proportion of organisations are including provision for working parents or carers of children (56% to a large or moderate extent), although for carers of elderly or ill relatives, another area that disproportionately affects women, the coverage is much more variable (65% offering little or no provision) (CIPD, 2022). Of 5000 UK workers sampled in 2023, those with caring responsibilities, who made up more than 40% of the survey (24% caring for children, 16% for related adults and 2% other adults), faced greater difficulties in achieving a positive work–life balance. They were more likely to experience difficulty in fulfilling outside commitments due to work, and vice versa, than noncarers (Young, 2023). Working flexibly in an ad hoc and informal way was easiest for those with childcare responsibilities compared to all those at work; however, in contrast, those caring for adult relatives found it more difficult.

During the pandemic, many employees took on caring responsibilities for the first time, helping to raise the profile of carers. Line managers can support carers by acknowledging their additional challenges and where possible, providing carers with the flexibility to respond as needed to balance caring with work in a healthy and sustainable way. This starts by creating an environment in which people feel comfortable to open up about their caring responsibilities and the impact on them. (Chapter 3 dives deeper on how to create a culture of trust under the section entitled 'the role of the line manager'.) Toolkits exist to help employers with practical tips to support careers at work, such as one developed by the Business in the Community (BITC, n.d.), a UK business-led membership organisation dedicated to responsible business.

TACKLING STIGMA

Pre-pandemic, emotional distress was common among hospital doctors, many of whom did not seek professional help or support from their colleagues, as they believed that they did not need it or were embarrassed to seek help and worried about confidentiality (Fridner et al. 2012). In fact, before the pandemic it was well known that the uptake of support among healthcare professionals was frequently stigmatised, which was a barrier to seeking support (Kinman & Teoh, 2018).

During the pandemic, despite high levels of various mental health problems amongst healthcare workers, they had comparable low rates of help-seeking behaviours and treatment for their mental problems (Cai et al., 2020). Stigma extends beyond the healthcare sector.

A 2020 study by BUPA (2020) found that 64% of board-level executives who experienced symptoms of mental ill health during the pandemic turned to potentially unhealthy coping mechanisms to deal with these issues, due to stigma. For instance, more than a third (36%) of business leaders in the UK turned to alcohol or drugs to deal with mental distress during the pandemic, with the vast majority admitting they self-medicated because they couldn't talk to anybody about their wellbeing concerns. The majority (78%) experienced symptoms such as fatigue, lack of motivation, mood swings and disturbed sleep. Despite widespread awareness of the mental health impact of the pandemic, stigma prevented many from seeking the help they needed. Two in five board-level executives (42%) believed that it would damage their reputation if it became known they were struggling, and a similar number were concerned about the impact on their professional or social reputation if they asked for help. As a result, only one in four of those affected (27%) had spoken to a medical professional.

The foundation of good leadership during the Covid-19 pandemic was found to include provision of a 'continuum of staff support' offering a range of initiatives, normalising feelings of distress, and encouraging their expression (Wu et al., 2020).

Collectively, these findings highlight the urgent need to reduce stigma, to enable staff to open up and seek help, identify mental health issues at an early stage, and provide timely support.

Tackling stigma requires effort focussed at the organisational, managerial and individual levels.

Organisational approach

The following case study outlines how Serco is normalising conversations about mental health:

Serco – Mental Health Literacy.

Finau Vucago – Wellbeing Manager and Kym Bancroft – Head of Health, Safety, Environment and Wellbeing

"The Serco AsPac approach to mental health literacy is always in the context of the workplace. We have taken a top-down approach in designing an education programme to increase mental health literacy and reduce stigma around mental ill health in the workplace. We take an integrated approach so there is just as much focus on prevention of harm and promotion of thriving, and not just mental ill-health."

With data in Australia showing that employee compensation claims for mental health were rising, Serco launched a three-year change management project in 2021 seeking to transform how Serco managed mental health. The focus was on increasing the mental health literacy amongst employees, starting with managers. There are approximately 750 managers in the AsPac region, and the aim is to have 80% of them through the programme.

The impact of the programme will be measured through the company survey looking at cultural shift and compensation claims.

British Telecom places emphasis on the importance of understanding what is really going on for employees:

BT Mental Health Campaign – 'Behind the Mask'.

Richard Caddis – Chief Medical Officer, BT

"BT developed the 'Behind the Mask' campaign in Autumn 2021 to drive forwards the BT agenda of being the company that is streets ahead of the rest in relation to creating a culture towards where there is no stigma regarding mental ill health."

Senior leader approach

Senior leaders and line managers play a powerful role in creating the right environment for people to open up. One way to do this is through sharing their own story. Those who may find this uncomfortable may find it easier to share when they are experiencing challenging situations in their lives, or how they proactively self-care in order to maintain their wellbeing. This will encourage others to do the same. The case study in Chapter 3 under the section on how line managers can 'create a culture of trust' through expressing vulnerability, (by David Gordon at GlaxoSmithKline), is an example of how a senior leader can impact the culture of their team, to create a more open and supportive work environment and a social movement that normalises mental health conversations.

THE VALUE OF EMPLOYEE RESOURCE GROUPS (ERGs) IN DRIVING THE DIVERSITY, EQUITY AND INCLUSION AGENDA

Employee Resource Groups (ERGs) are employee-led groups with shared characteristics that come together to advocate for their needs. Their aim is to foster a diverse and inclusive workplace. They have a strong influence within organisations and provide a platform to promote wellbeing, which is relevant amongst all ERGs. Utilising their reach and engagement with a significant proportion of the employee population, to drive the wellbeing agenda forward, is a significant opportunity not to be missed. For instance, using their communication channels to promote wellbeing topics, campaigns or training, encouraging their members to share their personal wellbeing stories at events and hosting panel sessions on wellbeing are ways to raise awareness of and access to EH&W resources.

The NHS CHECK survey found that colleagues provided more support than managers (76% vs 49%), which emphasises the significant role that each employee plays in support of one another, and the need for organisations and managers to create as many opportunities as possible for peer-to-peer interactions to develop supportive peer networks. ERGs are a great example of this, and they are to be found in many organisations. The purpose of these is to have a forum to discuss key challenges, seek support and raise the profile of the group and their needs. By supporting peer networks, organisations can play a greater role in enhancing the wellbeing, engagement and performance of their staff.

The following example from GlaxoSmithKline highlights the impact an ERG can make.

Employee Resource Groups: Addressing the intersectionality of Diversity, Equity and Inclusion; & health and wellbeing.

Serufusa Sekidde, an employee of the pharmaceutical company GSK, based in London. He is an Aspen New Voices Senior Fellow and a 2022 Empower Executive Role Model, run by Involve and Yahoo! Finance.

When I attended Harvard University in 2010, I joined a few other Black students at a Boston nightclub after the Harvard–Yale football game. We were there to celebrate a win, but soon, the racism we faced made us feel anything but celebratory.

The event began at 10 p.m. on 20 November. During the next hour, guests arrived and there were no problems inside or outside of the club, but at about 11:15 p.m., the nightclub management abruptly ended the event, asked the DJ to stop the music and the bouncers asked us all to leave. We were told there were "too many Black students, which would attract local gangbangers". We were all visibly shocked to hear this and some of us had to be held back to calm our justifiable anger in the moment. Vindicating us several months later, a court later ruled that was racial stereotyping and fined the club.

In those few months while we waited for the verdict, there were anecdotal reports that many Black students were deeply affected emotionally and psychologically. My own academic grades took a precipitous fall. Undeniably, this soured the Boston social experience for many of us who had come from outside, especially as we had few or no social networks to fall back on. And at that time in my life, I had not fully appreciated the value of counselling, so I didn't seek that out.

In the aftermath of that experience, I promised myself I would never stand by the wayside again – I had to fight for Diversity, Equity and Inclusion of anyone and everyone, regardless of race or ethnicity, sexual orientation, disability, or gender. Indeed, that was my inflection point, turning me into a vocal and visible social activist for racial, ethnic, and cultural diversity, equity and inclusion.

Over ten years later, I now co-lead EMBRACE Global, GSK's company-wide Employee Resource Group (ERG). Over the past two years I have been working with colleagues across 70+ countries to make sure our over 70,000 employees thrive by bringing all versions of themselves to work. EMBRACE started in GSK in 2017 with the objective of advocating for change on priority people and policy issues; celebrating ethnically diverse individuals and culture; as well as educating employees and management on race, ethnicity, and culture issues. We exist in an intersectional ecosystem with other ERGs that advocate on gender, sexuality and disability issues.

I'm proud to work for a company whose central strategy is to ensure that employees can contribute their best for patients who need our medicines and vaccines, while those employees navigate the myriad challenges that impact how they live, work, and relate to others. Best practice has shown that this includes, but is not limited to, adequate paid parental and sick leave, flexible work schedules and many other locally relevant policies.

What matters most is whether employees feel truly valued and supported. At the crux of that is the issue of Diversity, Equity and Inclusion. There is a clear expectation nowadays that companies must partner with Employee Resource Groups who will help educate both employees and management; agitate for employees and ensure appropriate celebration of the differences that make us a society.

GSK Employee Resource Groups play a pivotal role in the identification, development and implementation of relevant race and ethnicity; and LGBT+; gender and disability policies. We are routinely consulted during the development of the company's inclusion and diversity online trainings, which are now annual and mandatory for all employees. During the recent change of UK health insurance provider, we were consulted about which health benefits would matter most to ethnic minorities, LGBT+ colleagues, women and those living with disabilities. This strong partnership with HR and company leaders has ensured that employee wellbeing is viewed as a composite of their physical, mental, emotional, and financial health; work–life balance; and social equity.

A good example where this intersection comes to life is how companies now integrate wellbeing data with diversity information, for example with absence data which is now routinely broken down into age groups, ethnicity, gender and sexuality to see if there are any areas of concern and – this is where employee resource groups come in – to see if any targeted deep-dive analysis and supportive measures can be implemented. At the tail end of the recent Covid-19 epidemic, when companies were starting to encourage employees to return to their offices, we worked with management to ensure managers did this in a reasonable and inclusive way. Ethnic minorities are more likely to be part of multigenerational households in the UK, meaning that those employees were more likely to be apprehensive about returning to crowded places so soon because of the fear of endangering the health of elderly family members who lived with them. This was a good example to management and employee resource groups can work together to develop inclusive, flexible reward and benefit strategies that support employees from all backgrounds.

Managers, employees, and prospective employees all have distinct roles to play to bring to life this intersection between Diversity, Equity and Inclusion and employee wellbeing.

First, managers need to be aware that team members engagement in Employee Resource Groups is a win–win rather than a burden on their day job. In 2023, we in EMBRACE Global have run a sponsorship campaign where we have empowered colleagues with info and skills on how to better navigate career development resources; delivered trainings and talks on how to be more confident and persuasive – such as a recent one with Ms Makiziwe Mandela; and run a session on authenticity via the lens of inclusion and diversity with award-winning Nigerian-American Chimamanda Ngozi Adichie, which was attended by thousands of employees. These are all vital leadership skills that employees gain by being part of Employee Resource Groups, which not only improve their perception of wellbeing and self-worth, but are also directly transferable to their day jobs – especially for those working in cross-functional teams or those that need to deliver impact while with finite resources.

Second, current employees need to be aware of and, where possible, join Employee Resource Groups. They are a wonderful way of creating a sense of community with like-minded colleagues across the company. For the World Day of Cultural Diversity in May 2023, we in EMBRACE Global and five other race and ethnicity ERGs in GSK led a week-long campaign in which we encouraged colleagues from every part of the world to celebrate their culture by sharing pictures of the food they were eating that week, and their traditional clothes or national wear, as well as interesting facts about their culture. At our GSK global headquarters in London, we worked with our real estate team to decorate our canteens with flags from all the 70+ countries GSK has a presence and, on the day Ms Mandela spoke to the company, the staff restaurant served South African cuisine. In the USA, the race and ethnicity ERG Mosaic-led Africa Day celebrations, which included lessons about African culture and heritage – and the contribution African slaves and immigrants have made to the USA.

In choosing an ERG to join, what is important is picking an issue one is passionate about. The biggest and most important decision for most employees is how involved they'd like to be. It is up to you – but bear in mind that it needs to be clearly signposted to the ERG as well as your line manager in your day job. That's the key to success.

Lastly, prospective employees need to be aware that one of the best ways to judge a company's culture is to ask about its Diversity, Equity and Inclusion efforts as well as their wellbeing programmes. One of the ways of finding the right detail about this is to either ask HR or your hiring manager about this directly or, if possible and at the right stage of the recruitment process, to allow them to connect you to one of the leaders of the Employee Resource Groups. Only recently, a new GSK employee shared that they joined the company because we were the first large biopharma company in the FTSE 100 to publicly publish our ethnicity pay gap!

To be sure, there's no silver bullet for addressing wellbeing and DEI holistically, as each organisation's workforce is unique. It also takes time to see results; in any case, this will always be a moving target with increasing awareness and expectations on DEI as well as health and wellbeing. That is fine because there is mounting evidence that company success is inextricably tied to employee presence, engagement, and productivity. Without compassionate, inclusive, people-centred workplaces, employee health and wellbeing suffers, and so, in turn, does productivity. Employee Resource Groups are at the frontline of this change process, both as catalysts for change working in tandem with management and as referees and advocates who hold the mirror up to the organisation. Diversity, Equity and Inclusion should be the cultural norm and holistic health and wellbeing approaches are a must-have, not a nice to have.

Each one of us have our lived experience that we can bring to bear – like my Boston night club experience – and what leaders of employee resource groups like me do best is finding and channelling both our own experiences and those of our colleagues. We work hard to make sure they are heard and factored into tangible action in the companies where we work and the societies in which we live.

REACHING WORKERS THAT NEED HELP THE MOST

Frontline workers cannot access health and wellbeing support easily, therefore more effort is needed to reach them. Bringing wellbeing to them and integrating health and wellbeing into existing mandatory company processes are two ways to include all workers.

In 2021, a survey was commissioned by the American Psychological Association to explore Americans' attitudes towards the workplace and workforce. Adults who performed manual labour or worked in customer service, sales, or entertainment, were more likely to say that over the past month, mental or physical problems had kept them from achieving their goals at work. Regarding mental health problems, 42% of adults performing manual labour and 45% of adults working in customer service, sales, or entertainment reported suffering from such issues compared with 33% those working in administration, management, or desk jobs. The comparable figures for physical problems were 40% and 41%, respectively compared with 30%. When it came to job level, lower-level employees were more likely to experience negative impacts of work-related stress (67% frontline and 64% mid-level vs. 54% upper-level) (American Psychological Association, 2021).

Reaching those workers who have the greatest need for EH&W support requires an approach involving all levels of the workforce – most importantly, line managers and the employees themselves. Bringing wellbeing to hard to reach workers will allow them to access the services they need in a timely way.

The below example shows how SUEZ integrated health and wellbeing content into existing mandatory programmes to ensure that all frontline workers were made aware of relevant topics. Conferences, site roadshows and campaigns ensure ongoing reach.

SUEZ recycling and recovery UK.

Dr Tracey Leghorn – Chief Business Services Officer and Natalie Sáenz, SW Regional Communications Manager

Data analysis in the early stages of Covid-19 identified that our workforce was experiencing higher levels of stress and anxiety. Our frontline workers had been designated as key workers by the government and continued to provide essential waste services to the nation during challenging times.

We identified that an effective way to reach over 1500 frontline employees was through our Driver (Certificate of Professional Competence) CPC course. The CPC is mandatory professional development required to retain their driving certificate. We created a bespoke wellbeing course covering areas such as mental health, stress, nutrition and alcohol use specifically for our drivers. This course received approval from the regulator, Jaupt. We believe this is the first time that wellbeing has been the focus of a Driver CPC course. All SUEZ drivers have been attending this training since October 2021, delivered by our in-house training team.

To support our focus on elevating the importance of wellbeing, in line with safety, in 2022 our board decided to incorporate a mandatory requirement into the company bonus scheme for all eligible employees to have a wellbeing and inclusion objective as part of their annual performance and development review. Furthermore, that their actions against this objective must be recorded in our People and Planet app so that they can be captured, and the data used to inform our future programme.

Wellbeing and Inclusion also featured at our employee conferences in May 2022 and with the support of the board and senior managers, we organised our first dedicated Wellbeing and Inclusion Conference. 80 delegate places were made open, 40 of which were ring-fenced to frontline employees who were nominated by their regional managers. The conference was a huge success and has now become an annual event.

Our efforts to reach frontline workers continue with a Health MOT Roadshow, which visited a number of sites. The Roadshow was created collaboratively with our occupational health provider and supported by our Wellbeing and Inclusion Ambassadors. It provided instant results and support on issues such as diabetes, heart health, BMI and blood pressure. The feedback and benefit to our frontline workforce has been fantastic with one delegate saying: "I couldn't believe my cholesterol level was 8.9, the referral to see my doctor was a bit of a shock but within 3 months with diet and lifestyle changes I managed to get my cholesterol level down to 6.9 and now 9 months on it's down to 5.1. Without the Roadshow I would have been totally unaware of the changes I needed to make."

Our 2023 roadshow scheduled for later this year links closely with the Movember campaign and will include a lifestyle questionnaire to raise awareness and help identify the risk factors of prostate cancer. This, together with other activities throughout November, provides a month-long focus on men's health and wellbeing.

Our wellness webinars continue to be held every Friday and have featured subjects ranging from healthy eating to the restorative powers of exercise and coping mechanisms for anxiety. Aligned with our wellness principle that wellness extends into all aspects of our lives, they cover issues well beyond the confines of the workplace. Where possible we've shared these on LinkedIn as part of our commitment to social value, giving access outside of our workplace to this fantastic wellbeing resource. By analysing trends and listening to feedback from our people, they continue to shape our programme. We have produced a wellness webinar catalogue with QR codes to enable our frontline colleagues to 'watch back' and all of our Wellness for All webinars and events are advertised on our me. SUEZ app used by all our frontline workers.

On the ground, wellbeing initiatives are increasingly popular with an increase in wellbeing webinar attendance, employee benefits usage, wellbeing coffee mornings, 'Time to talk' sessions and wellbeing areas being created on sites. Wellbeing conversations are becoming the norm, as they should be, and we know through our recent Employee Engagement survey that our people feel supported and know that SUEZ are there to support them in their time of need.

By identifying which groups have the greatest need as a result of higher risks of poor wellbeing, organisations can take a proactive and tailored approach, to prevent or reduce the severity of adverse impact to health, wellbeing, engagement and productivity and help their employees thrive.

ACTIONS

1. Consult credible health and wellbeing expertise to identify employee groups at greater risk of poor wellbeing. Take a targeted and tailored approach to reach these groups most at need.

2. Line manager training must include understanding which groups of employees may experience poorer levels of wellbeing and how to support them.
3. As a line manager, invest time to understand the individual circumstances of employees to allow you to take a personalised and inclusive approach to their needs.
4. Social support plays a significant role in mental wellbeing. Relatively simple ways to encourage this within organisations include organising networking events, setting up peer-to-peer support networks to provide opportunities for employees to interact, and creating and sponsoring Employee Resource Groups.
5. Normalise mental health conversations by keeping mental health on the agenda during individual and team conversations and town halls, sharing stories, campaigns and programmes to improve mental health literacy and raising awareness of support services available.

REFERENCES

Achor, S., Kellerman, G.R., Reece, A., & Robichaux, A. (2018). America's loneliest workers, according to research. *Harvard Business Review* March, *19*(1), 13–28.

Adams, J.G., & Walls, R.M. (2020). Supporting the health care workforce during the COVID-19 global epidemic. *JAMA, 323*(15), 1439–1440.

American Psychological Association. (2021). *Compounding pressure 2021: Americans' attitudes toward the workplace and workforce.* Retrieved November 27, from https://www.apa.org/pubs/reports/work-well-being/compounding-pressure-2021

Aughterson, H., McKinlay, A.R., Fancourt, D., & Burton, A. (2021). Psychosocial impact on frontline health and social care professionals in the UK during the COVID-19 pandemic: A qualitative interview study. *BMJ Open, 11*(2), e047353.

Beesley, V.L., Price, M.A., & Webb, P.M. Australian Ovarian Cancer Study—Quality of Life Study Investigators. (2011). Loss of lifestyle: Health behaviour and weight changes after becoming a caregiver of a family member diagnosed with ovarian cancer. *Support Care Cancer, 19*(12), 1949–1956.

Brans, K., Koval, P., Verduyn, P., & Lim, Y.L. (2013). The regulation of negative and positive affect in daily life. *Emotion, 13*(5), 926–939.

Bupa. (2020). Your wellbeing - Our research. Retrieved November 27, from https://www.bupaglobal.com/ar/your-wellbeing/our-research/self-medication.

Business in the Community. (n.d.). *Supporting Carers in the Workplace. A practical guide for employers*. The Prince's Responsible Business Network. Retrieved November 27, from https://www.bitc.org.uk/toolkit/supporting-carers-in-the-workplace/

Cai, Q., Feng, H., Huang, J., Wang, M., Wang, Q., Lu, X., … Liu, Y. (2020). The mental health of frontline and non-frontline medical workers during the coronavirus disease 2019 (COVID-19) outbreak in China: A case-control study. *Journal of Affective Disorders, 275*, 210–215.

CIPD. (2022). Health and Wellbeing at Work Report 2022. Retrieved November 27, from https://www.cipd.org/globalassets/media/comms/news/ahealth-wellbeing-work-report-2022_tcm18-108440.pdf

Clarkson, C., Scott, H.R., Hegarty, S., Souliou, E., Bhundia, R., Gnanapragasam, S., … Lamb, D. (2023). 'You get looked at like you're failing': A reflexive thematic analysis of experiences of mental health and wellbeing support for NHS staff. *Journal of Health Psychology, 28*, 13591053221140255.

Frenkel, M.O., Giessing, L., Egger-Lampl, S., Hutter, V., Oudejans, R.R.D., Kleygrewe, L., Jaspaert, E., Plessner, H. (2021). The impact of the COVID-19 pandemic on European police officers: Stress, demands, and coping resources. *Journal of Criminal Justice, 72*, 101756.

Fridner, A., Belkic, K., Marini, M., Sendén, M. G., & Schenck-Gustafsson, K. (2012). Why don't academic physicians seek needed professional help for psychological distress? *Swiss Medical Weekly, 142*(2930), 13626.

Fujiwara, D., Dolan, P., Lawton, R., Behzadnejad, F., Lagarde, A., Maxwell, C., & Peytrignet, S. (2020). *Wellbeing costs of COVID-19 in the UK*. Simetrica-Jacobs London School of Economics and Political Science. https://www.ceci.org.uk/the-wellbeing-costs-of-covid-19-in-the-uk/#:~:text=The%20costs%20of%20the%20COVID,53)%20per%20adult%20each%20day

Gilleen, J., Santaolalla, A., Valdearenas, L., Salice, C., & Fusté, M. (2021). Impact of the COVID-19 pandemic on the mental health and well-being of UK healthcare workers. *BJPsych Open, 7*(3), e88. doi:10.1192/bjo.2021.42

Giovannetti, E.R., Wolff, J.L., Frick, K.D., & Boult, C. (2009). Construct validity of the work productivity and activity impairment questionnaire across informal caregivers of chronically ill older patients. *Value in Health, 12*(6), 1011–1017.

Hegarty, S., Lamb, D., Stevelink, S.A., Bhundia, R., Raine, R., Doherty, M.J., … Wessely, S. (2022). 'It hurts your heart': Frontline healthcare worker experiences of moral injury during the COVID-19 pandemic. *European Journal of Psychotraumatology, 13*(2), 2128028.

Imo, U.O. (2017). Burnout and psychiatric morbidity among doctors in the UK: A systematic literature review of prevalence and associated factors. *BJPsych Bulletin, 41*, 197–204.

Jia, R., Ayling, K., Chalder, T., Massey, A., Broadbent, E., Coupland, C., & Vedhara, K. (2020). Mental health in the UK during the COVID-19 pandemic: Cross-sectional analyses from a community cohort study. *BMJ Open, 10*(9), e040620.

Kinman, G., & Teoh, K. (2018). What could make a difference to the mental health of UK doctors? A review of the research evidence.

Labrague, L.J. (2021). Psychological resilience, coping behaviours and social support among health care workers during the COVID-19 pandemic: A systematic review of quantitative studies. *Journal of Nursing Management, 29*(7), 1893–1905.

Labrague, L.J., & de Los Santos, J. (2020). COVID-19 anxiety among frontline nurses: Predictive role of organizational support, personal resilience and social support. *Journal of Nursing Management, 28*(7), 1653–1661.

Lai, J., Ma, S., Wang, Y., Cai, Z., Hu, J., Wei, N., … Hu, S. (2020). Factors associated with mental health outcomes among health care workers exposed to coronavirus disease 2019. *JAMA Network Open, 3*(3), e203976–e203976.

Lamb, D., Gnanapragasam, S., Greenberg, N., Bhundia, R., Carr, E., Hotopf, M., … Wessely, S. (2021a). Psychosocial impact of the COVID-19 pandemic on 4378 UK healthcare workers and ancillary staff: Initial baseline data from a cohort study collected during the first wave of the pandemic. *Occupational and Environmental Medicine, 78*(11), 801–808.

Lamb, D., Greenberg, N., Hotopf, M., Raine, R., Razavi, R., Bhundia, R., … Stevelink, S. (2021b). NHS CHECK: Protocol for a cohort study investigating the psychosocial impact of the COVID-19 pandemic on healthcare workers. *BMJ Open, 11*(6), e051687.

Lee, S.H., Juang, Y.Y., Su, Y.J., Lee, H.L., Lin, Y.H., & Chao, C.C. (2005). Facing SARS: Psychological impacts on SARS team nurses and psychiatric services in a Taiwan general hospital. *General Hospital Psychiatry, 27*(5), 352–358.

Liu, Y., & Aungsuroch, Y. (2019). Work stress, perceived social support, self-efficacy and burnout among Chinese registered nurses. *Journal of Nursing Management, 27*(7), 1445–1453.

Liu, Y., Gayle, A.A., Wilder-Smith, A., & Rocklöv, J. (2020). The reproductive number of COVID-19 is higher compared to SARS coronavirus. *Journal of Travel Medicine, 27*(2), 1–4.

Luo, M., Guo, L., Yu, M., & Wang, H. (2020). The psychological and mental impact of coronavirus disease 2019 (COVID-19) on medical staff and the general public–A systematic review and meta-analysis. *Psychiatry Research, 291*, 113190.

Marmot, M., Friel, S., Bell, R., Houweling, T. A., & Taylor, S. (2008). Closing the gap in a generation: Health equity through action on the social determinants of health. *The Lancet, 372*(9650), 1661–1669.

McAlonan, G.M., Lee, A.M., Cheung, V., Cheung, C., Tsang, K.W., Sham, P.C., … Wong, J.G. (2007). Immediate and sustained psychological impact of an emerging infectious disease outbreak on health care workers. *The Canadian Journal of Psychiatry*, *52*(4), 241–247.

Norris-Green, M., & Gifford, J. (2021). *CIPD good work index 2021*. London: Chartered Institute of Personnel and Development.

McSweeney, R. (2020). *Coronavirus and Key Workers in the UK*. Office for National Statistics. https://www.ons.gov.uk/employmentandlabourmarket/peopleinwork/earningsandworkinghours/articles/coronavirusandkeyworker sintheuk/2020-05-15

Padmanathan, P., Lamb, D., Scott, H., Stevelink, S., Greenberg, N., Hotopf, M., … Moran, P. (2023). Suicidal thoughts and behaviour among healthcare workers in England during the COVID-19 pandemic: A longitudinal study. *PLoS ONE*, *18*(6), e0286207.

Paul, E., Mak, H.W., Fancourt, D., & Bu, F. (2021). Comparing mental health trajectories of four different types of key workers with non-key workers: A 12-month follow-up observational study of 21,874 adults in England during the COVID-19 pandemic. *Med R xiv*, 2021-04.

Pieh, C., Budimir, S., & Probst, T. (2020). The effect of age, gender, income, work, and physical activity on mental health during coronavirus disease (COVID-19) lockdown in Austria. *Journal of Psychosomatic Research*, *136*, 110186.

Scott, H.R., Stevelink, S.A., Gafoor, R., Lamb, D., Carr, E., Bakolis, I., … Wessely, S. (2023). Prevalence of post-traumatic stress disorder and common mental disorders in health-care workers in England during the COVID-19 pandemic: A two-phase cross-sectional study. *The Lancet Psychiatry*, *10*(1), 40–49.

Sim, M.R. (2020). The COVID-19 pandemic: Major risks to healthcare and other workers on the front line. *Occupational and Environmental Medicine*, *77*(5), 281–282.

Stenberg, U., Ruland, C.M., & Miaskowski, C. (2010). Review of the literature on the effects of caring for a patient with cancer. *Psycho-oncology*, *19*(10), 1013–1025.

Swanberg, J.E. (2006). Making it work: Informal caregiving, cancer, and employment. *Journal of Psychosocial Oncology*, *24*(3), 1–18.

Toh, W.L., Meyer, D., Phillipou, A., Tan, E.J., Van Rheenen, T.E., Neill, E., & Rossell, S.L. (2021). Mental health status of healthcare versus other essential workers in Australia amidst the COVID-19 pandemic: Initial results from the collate project. *Psychiatry Research*, *298*, 113822.

Varga, T.V., Bu, F., Dissing, A.S., Elsenburg, L.K., Bustamante, J.J.H., Matta, J., … Rod, N.H. (2021). Loneliness, worries, anxiety, and precautionary behaviours in response to the COVID-19 pandemic: A longitudinal analysis of 200,000 Western and Northern Europeans. *The Lancet Regional Health – Europe, 2.*

Vindrola-Padros, C., Andrews, L., Dowrick, A., Djellouli, N., Fillmore, H., Gonzalez, E.B., ... Johnson, G. (2020). Perceptions and experiences of healthcare workers during the COVID-19 pandemic in the UK. *BMJ Open, 10*(11), e040503.

Williams, T., Davis, J., Figueira, C., & Vizard, T. (2021). Coronavirus and depression in adults, Great Britain: January to March 2021. Office for National Statistics, https://www.ons.gov.uk/peoplepopulationandcommunity/wellbeing/articles/coronavirusanddepressioninadultsgreatbritain/januarytomarch2021

Williamson, V., Lamb, D., Hotopf, M., Raine, R., Stevelink, S., Wessely, S., ... Greenberg, N. (2023). Moral injury and psychological wellbeing in UK healthcare staff. *Journal of Mental Health, 32*(5), 890–898.

Wong, E., Ho, K.F., Wong, S.Y.S., Cheung, A.W.L., & Yeoh, E.K. (2020). Workplace safety and coronavirus disease (COVID-19) pandemic: Survey of employees. *Bull World Health Organ, 98,* 150.

Wu, A.W., Connors, C., & Everly Jr, G.S. (2020). COVID-19: peer support and crisis communication strategies to promote institutional resilience. *Annals of Internal Medicine, 172*(12), 822–823.

Wu, P., Fang, Y., Guan, Z., Fan, B., Kong, J., Yao, Z., ... Hoven, C.W. (2009). The psychological impact of the SARS epidemic on hospital employees in China: Exposure, risk perception, and altruistic acceptance of risk. *The Canadian Journal of Psychiatry, 54*(5), 302–311.

Xiong, J., Lipsitz, O., Nasri, F., Lui, L.M., Gill, H., Phan, L., ... McIntyre, R.S. (2020). Impact of COVID-19 pandemic on mental health in the general population: A systematic review. *Journal of Affective Disorders, 277,* 55–64.

Young, J. (2023). *CIPD good work index 2023: summary report.* London: Chartered Institute of Personnel and Development. https://www.cipd.org/globalassets/media/knowledge/knowledge-hub/reports/2023-pdfs/2023-good-work-index-summary-report-8407.pdf

THE FLEXIBLE WORKER

Flexible working positively impacts engagement and performance (with some caveats)

Key messages

1. There has been a relatively recent paradigm shift in our perception of hybrid working. It is now mostly seen by employers as enabling employees to maintain, and possibly improve, their productivity. This shift, from an input-orientated (where people work and counting the numbers of hours they work) to an output-focused approach for workers conducting office-based roles, has been profound.

2. Leaders that are questioning the positive link between hybrid working and productivity and putting efforts into reversing the trend need to ask themselves whether they need to engage existing employees and attract and retain the best talent, and, if so, whether they are able to accept hybrid working as the new norm, that overall has benefits for individuals and the organisation.

3. Having the opportunity to work flexibly enhances employee well-being, work–life balance, and overall life satisfaction, all of which contribute towards improving engagement and performance. For roles where it is possible, a mix of remote and non-remote work is associated with better health and wellbeing outcomes and performance versus either alone.

DOI: 10.4324/9781003124979-5

4. While choice and flexibility in where and how people work can be beneficial for wellbeing, adverse consequences, such as isolation, and achieving a positive work–life balance, can be a reality for certain groups of people, such as women, who are more likely than men to work remotely. Additionally, while individual task performance remains high, productivity in relation to tasks that require collaboration can be negatively impacted by home working.

5. Organisations can enable employees to maintain high levels of wellbeing and productivity when working remotely through providing the right equipment, technological solutions, providing opportunities to connect, supporting physical and mental health, and creating an inclusive environment.

6. Employers must look to address inequalities between office and onsite workers with regard to flexible working opportunities, for instance, identifying how onsite workers can be given more choice, and prevent potential unintended gender inequality brought about by a more visibly male-dominated workforce, through supporting female population career progression.

7. Clear guidance set and communicated by employers will help clarify when in-person interactions would be most effective, and therefore recommended, or even expected. Managers must be supported to have honest conversations with their staff on expectations.

8. This shift in ways of working will demand new management approaches to support the positive health and wellbeing, inclusion, and motivation of those working remotely. Building manager skills to manage remote workers should be a key consideration.

THE PRE-PANDEMIC POSITION ON FLEXIBLE WORKING

In general, the consensus prior to the pandemic amongst leaders and managers, was that flexible working (including remote working) negatively impacted both engagement and productivity. This was a result of various factors, including societal norms in relation to 'normal' practices, beliefs around the environment in which employees are most productive, employer expectations and the evidence available. The lack of trust that some managers had in their staff to work effectively from home often resulted in micromanagement, and workers feeling mistrusted, despite emerging evidence to support the benefits of working remotely. For instance, a finding that the more flexibility employees had on where they worked, the greater autonomy and work–life balance they experienced, which increased their wellbeing (Hoeven and Zoonen, 2015). When employees feel that they have control in how they do their work, it enables them to better manage their work–life balance (Beckers et al., 2012). Research reveals, unsurprisingly, that the enhanced work–life balance that remote working facilitates, improves levels of job satisfaction, engagement (Felstead & Henseke, 2017) and worker mental health (Kotera et al., 2020). Increased autonomy is a key component of motivation at work and is also linked to reduced levels of stress (Van Steenbergen et al., 2018). When we are more motivated, our work performance is enhanced (Pritchard & Payne, 2003). An experiment on flexible work practices over nine months was carried out at a Chinese travel agency with more than 16,000 employees, in which call centre agents were randomly assigned to either working from home or working in the office, as was normal practice. At the end of the experiment, call centre agents who were working from home experienced fewer negative and more positive emotions, less exhaustion, and reported a higher overall life satisfaction compared to call centre agents who were working in the office. Of real significance was that working from home also led to a 13% increase in performance, of which 9% was attributed to working more minutes per shift (due to fewer breaks and sick days) and 4% due to taking more calls per minute (due to a quieter working environment). Interestingly, staff turnover halved. The company was estimated to save approximately US$2,000 annually per call centre agent working from home. As a result of this study, the scheme was implemented across the entire workforce. This change almost doubled performance gains, to 22% (Bloom et al., 2015). Flexible work practices are thought to allow employees the space to better manage their responsibilities at home which, in turn, improves their ability to devote more effort to their jobs (Moen et al., 2011). While this strong evidence base may start to imply a 'just do it' approach, less favourable experiences have also been observed. For instance, for some, autonomy levels can actually reduce when working flexibly, as a result of increased expectations regarding the availability of employees, resulting in an 'always on' phenomenon (Mazmanian et al., 2013) that leads to a compromised work–life balance, due to blurred boundaries between work and personal lives (Demerouti et al., 2014). Personal behaviours can also play a part. Remote workers can tend to overwork to reciprocate the permitted flexibility (Kelliher & Anderson, 2010), for instance, exchanging emails during non-working hours, a practice that has been linked to stress for both the worker and the recipient (Chesley, 2014). With these conflicting research outcomes pre-pandemic and no real impetus for things to change at scale, remote working was rarely available or offered.

THE PARADIGM SHIFT IN FLEXIBLE WORKING PRACTICES AS A RESULT OF THE COVID-19 PANDEMIC

The International Monetary Fund (International Monetary Fund, 2020) estimated in October 2020, that the World Gross Domestic product (GDP) would drop by 4.4% as a result of the containment measures taken to reduce the spread of Covid-19, with countries particularly hit by the virus, such as Italy, experiencing a drop of over 10%. This expected drop in GDP was estimated to be larger if significant numbers of people would not be able to work remotely from home, where their roles permitted this. Workplaces shifted ways of working, where possible, to remote working, with virtually no warning. The Covid-19 pandemic facilitated a seismic shift in how we practice and perceive home working across the globe. The UK's professional body for HR and people development, the CIPD, reported that in 2010 approximately 3% of workers were working from home all the time. This rose gradually to around 5% from January–March 2020, before the impact of the pandemic. However, after that point, the figures then rose rapidly in response to the UK government's guidance that all workers (who were able to) should work from home. Between October and December 2020, those working from home all of the time was at 10% (CIPD, 2023). This trend has grown exponentially throughout the Covid-19 pandemic, when many organisations went from having a modest percentage of team members working virtually, to the entire workforce working from home.

The following examples, from UK Policing and Devon and Cornwall Police, demonstrates how accelerating the opportunity to work flexibly shifted mindsets, almost overnight.

UK Policing.

Andy Rhodes, OBE and Dr Ian Hesketh

Flexible working and the adoption of technological solutions to facilitate had, hitherto, made slow progress in policing. Much of this stems from a cultural reluctance to loosen up management oversight. Covid-19 forced us to do what we should have been doing already, and the subsequent business continuity benefits have driven a paradigm shift across the service. Questions started to be asked about the shape of capital investment programmes. Why are we investing in a multi-storey car park to solve parking problems when we have proven the benefits of hybrid remote working for so many of our people? Why not shift that funding into enabling technologies instead?

Devon and Cornwall Police.

Professor John Harrison – Chief Medical Officer

The positive impact of Covid in the workplace has been that flexible working is now more acceptable than pre-Covid, with mindsets changing to one where people can be productive from home. One of the benefits the force has seen is that people are in fact spending more on their job without the usual commute.

As with the examples above, employers' perceptions of home-working changed. The CIPD's 2021 survey on 2000 employers, and in-depth interviews with seven organisations in different sectors, demonstrated that perceived productivity benefits of homeworking appear to have increased during the pandemic. This seems to be increasing with time. Employers in 2021 were more likely to say that the shift to homeworking has boosted productivity (33%) than they were in June 2020 (28%) (CIPD, 2021). The survey found that employers were also less likely to say that increased homeworking has decreased productivity (23%) compared to a year prior to the survey, suggesting that employers have had a significant net productivity benefit over that period. Encouragingly, more than two-thirds (71%) of employers said that the increase in homeworking either boosted or made no difference to productivity. Overall, there were positive experiences of working flexibly, with benefits to both employees and organisations.

BENEFITS OF WORKING FLEXIBLY

Overall, employees value greater autonomy, less time commuting, a better quality of life and greater perceived productivity from working remotely. A study on 436 Lithuanian remote workers found that advantages were related to the flexibility of work organisation (the possibility to choose worktime and workplace, and time saved in commuting (Raišienė et al., 2020)). In a study on researchers, having greater flexibility in daily routine and working hours, was reported as a bonus when working from home, as was having more time for personal activities because of not commuting (Kappel et al., 2021). The vast majority (83%) perceived positive changes in their daily routine during lockdown, such as spending more time talking/engaging with family and friends than normal (45%), an improved work–life balance (34%), and having time to catch up on work that was stalled because other tasks previously took priority (31% of respondents). Similar results were found following a survey of 2595 remote workers in New Zealand, where productivity was similar or higher than pre-lockdown, and 89% of professionals wanted to continue to work from home on at least one day per month. Working from home led to a drastic saving of time otherwise allocated to daily commuting, a higher degree of flexibility, and increased savings (Walton et al., 2020). It was not just those with family responsibilities who had positive experiences. A questionnaire survey looking at the effectiveness of greater online working as a result of the Covid-19 pandemic, was conducted on 200 millennial generation employees at one of Honda's motorcycle dealers in Jakarta, Indonesia. The results showed that e-training, e-leadership, and work–life balance had positive effects on work motivation. Additionally, e-training, e-leadership, work–life balance, and work motivation had positive effects on employee performance (Wolor et al., 2020). From the CIPD's 2021 Good Work Index survey of more than 5000 workers across the UK, less positive responses were reported on overall health and wellbeing by those spending *all* of their time working from home or *never* working from home; therefore a mix of in-work and home working days may be ideal for positive wellbeing (Norris-Green & Gifford, 2021). A global study on software engineers based predominantly in the UK and US who were working remotely found that wellbeing and productivity were positively associated (Russo et al., 2021). Therefore, neglecting employee wellbeing may negatively impact productivity. Positive predictors of wellbeing included the quality of social contacts and negative predictors of productivity were boredom and distractions.

During times of significant social restrictions, technologies providing social exchange received a spike in demand, and social connectedness appeared to become especially important for coping. Technology enabled greater reach, to better support those working from home. Many organisations utilised technology to deliver wellbeing support, which led to greater awareness of and access to resources. The following example illustrates how Devon and Cornwall Police brought this concept to life.

Devon and Cornwall Police – Virtual wellbeing support.

Professor John Harrison – Chief Medical Officer

Embracing technology – Covid transformed the use of technology throughout the organisation which adapted rapidly to using Teams and Skype. The role of Teams for promoting and delivering wellbeing was crucial.

Delivering H&W virtually – Virtual wellbeing conference/festival in October 2020, which was a week-long series of events included internal and external speakers, webinars and talk cafés. The talk cafés were so popular that they continued into 2021 and have proved to be effective in facilitating conversations. The success of the festival was the reach as accessibility was facilitated by having it virtual (you only needed a computer), recording the event which could then be seen on demand. The 2021 annual Wellfest – an award-winning initiative – had 1700 requests for invitations.

CHALLENGES OF WORKING FLEXIBLY

For certain employee groups, flexible working proved to be, and continues to be, a challenging experience. Awareness of these groups and what they need will enable managers to support them to be at their best. We now consider individual and team level challenges.

At the employee level

Exclusion and Loneliness

Prior to the pandemic, people working from home tended to report less inclusion than those within traditional work arrangements (Morganson et al., 2010), which negatively impacted individual and team performance. Restrictions imposed by the pandemic, such as social/physical distancing measures and the change to remote work environments, increased employees' feelings of loneliness and social exclusion (Kopp, 2020; Robinson, 2020). Many felt a lack of inclusion as well as sense of belonging, particularly those who were childless (Miller, 2020) and single (Smith, 2020), which impacted their mental health and wellbeing as well as organisational productivity. People who feel they have less social support and perceive themselves to be lonelier, have poorer mental health outcomes, and increased morbidity and mortality (Wang et al., 2018). Loneliness is a significant risk factor for physical and mental ill-health (Tiwari, 2013). It is associated with physical (e.g. higher risk of cardiovascular disease, compromised immunity and shortened life span (Holt-Lunstad et al., 2015) as well as mental health consequences (Raheel, 2014). Conversely, social relationships, both private and professional, were key factors in coping with lockdown challenges (Nitschke et al., 2021). Learnings from these experiences are that workplace mental health interventions aimed at keeping employees connected and encouraging social interactions, that are inclusive of remote workers, will help address these feeling of isolation and exclusion. In the UK, those who were at much greater risk of Covid-19 were defined on medical grounds as extremely vulnerable to the disease, and were advised by the government to stay at home to shield themselves. As a result, this group experienced isolation to a greater extent (Lai et al., 2020). At Wrightington Wigan and Leigh Teaching Hospitals NHS Foundation Trust, employees who were shielding were supported to keep connected through the efforts of their Wellbeing Teams, Staff Engagement colleagues and their Employee Champions who also led activities to keep the wider workforce connected.

Wrightington Wigan and Leigh Teaching Hospitals NHS Foundation Trust – keeping staff connected.

Zoe Garnett – Staff Wellbeing Manager

During the pandemic, the wellbeing team called S4W (Steps4Wellness) developed a range of wellbeing resources that could easily be accessed by those of our staff who had been deemed Clinically Extremely Vulnerable and therefore had to shield. These resources included reading materials about maintaining their own wellbeing and an online training package developed by our team "Building personal resilience". The resources also suggested ideas, apps, game platforms and other elements of social media to enable them to keep socially connected with their colleagues, family and friends despite not seeing them physically.

The team also supported listening events run by our Staff Engagement colleagues for this group of shielding staff. Often wellbeing concerns were aired at these forums and so we were on hand to be able to offer advice and signpost to further avenues of support as necessary. Just being part of a group who had had similar experiences through the pandemic and being able to meet up regularly albeit it virtually gave people some of the social connections they had been missing.

Our Steps4Wellness Champions developed some innovative ways to keep their teams motivated and connected during these unprecedented times of pressure, including virtual duck races, team quizzes, team step challenges, weight loss groups and also, for those in work, a way to let go of the day at the end of shift before going home to recharge, the "Check in before you check out" initiative.

This example also highlights the power in harnessing the passion of employees to support the wellbeing of their colleagues. This is explored further in Chapter 6.

Work–life balance

Those working from home report more positive overall work–life balance; however, a deeper dive reveals that while remote workers report better *access* to flexible working options, they may not report a better balance between work and non-work commitments. For example, those working from home all the time, or part of the time, were more likely to say they found it difficult to relax in their personal time due to their job (29% and 27% of those working fully or partly at home respectively, compared with 18% of those going into work) (Norris-Green & Gifford, 2021). Clear boundaries between work and home are important for psychological detachment, which can lower levels of stress and exhaustion (Sonnentag, 2012). Even those who have adjusted well to remote working conditions post-pandemic, have been challenged by the inability to seek alternative workspaces, such as cafés or co-working spaces, outside of the home. This has adversely affected the segmentation between work and private life, leading to greater difficulties in "unplugging" from work demands (Chawla et al., 2020). To address this, employees need to set clear boundaries of when they will and will not work, and line managers must discuss work–life balance and social connection regularly during one-to-one meetings.

The impact of greater use of technology

While technology has been fundamental to business continuity and maintaining connections, there have been many challenges associated with greater use of technology. Being on video calls can set up an evaluative context, where employees feel judged for how they look and what can be seen around them, which can cause stress. Selecting a background from video software or agreeing to go off video can be helpful. Continuous back-to-back video calls involves staring intensely at screens, with the reluctance to look away, even momentarily, out of feeling that one may be perceived as not giving sufficient attention, despite this being normal in face-to-face settings. It can lead to eye fatigue and headaches. Encouraging people to use non-video means to communicate, when screens are not needed, to take advantage of walk and talk meetings and educating employees on desk exercises as a way to prevent eye and musculoskeletal strain can help address these challenges.

Women and hybrid working

Women, in particular, appreciated the opportunity to work from home during the pandemic to allow for a greater flexibility, to help manage conflicting demands. Within couples where both partners worked, women were less likely to have kept working in their usual workplace than men (23% of women as opposed to 33% of their partners) and 44% of working women kept their jobs by working from home (versus 30% of men) (Del Boca et al., 2020). Women were therefore much more likely to work from home and manage conflicting demands. Working women with young children found balancing work and family more difficult during the pandemic, particularly when their partners continued to work outside the home during the pandemic. Organisations that are diversifying their workforces, by recruiting more women into a variety of roles, must address their needs to achieve a healthy work–life balance, and additionally counterbalance the more visibly male-dominated workforce, to ensure gender equality.

At the team level

Trust

At a team level, trust and collaboration need greater attention when working remotely. Working as a virtual team brings an additional layer of communication challenges. Reduced nonverbal communication and poorer communication quality in general can, in some cases, lead to anxiety, confusion, and miscommunication among employees (Daim et al. 2012). These employee experiences can impact trust, resulting in the level of trust in virtual teams generally lower than among physically communicating colleagues (Benetytė & Jatuliavičienė, 2013). Lack of trust can become an obstacle to effective execution of virtual work; therefore within virtual teams, who may have incomplete knowledge of all team members, ensuring a high degree of trust is much more important than in traditional ones (Mogale & Sutherland, 2010) and reinforces the importance of investing in building psychological safety. (The role of the line manager is detailed in Chapter 3.)

Collaboration

While employees in general feel they perform equally well at home and in the office, when conducting tasks that require collaboration, they are more satisfied doing so in person (Global Work Analytics, n.d.).

An employee attitudes to remote working survey was conducted on 1200 professionals who were employed before and during Covid-19 in 2020 in the US, Germany, and India (Boston Consulting Group, 2020). Participants were conducting roles where they could work remotely, such as analysts, engineers, HR personnel, teachers, and healthcare providers. The survey found that employees perceived that their productivity predominantly stayed the same or even improved and 75% of employees said that during the first few months of the pandemic they had been able to maintain or improve productivity on their individual tasks (such as analysing data, writing presentations, and executing administrative tasks). The number, however, was lower on *collaborative tasks*, with only 51% feeling they were able to maintain or improve their productivity. Collaborative work seems more challenging virtually and appears to generate most concern among employers, many of whom assume teams need to meet in person to collaborate. In this study, employees felt that four factors supported productivity during collaborative tasks, whether working remotely or onsite: social connectivity, mental health, physical health, and workplace tools. In fact, 79% of respondents who indicated they are satisfied or doing better on all four of these factors said they have been able to maintain or improve productivity on collaborative tasks. Managers should therefore focus on supporting employee health, developing and maintaining workplace connections and ensuring employees have the right workplace tools.

The following example from Transport for London shows how providing workplace tools and equipment enabled employees to remain productive.

Transport for London SHOE Project – Provision of workplace tools.

Dr Samantha Philips – Head of Health and Wellbeing

Following a wellbeing survey in June/July 2020 which was prompted by the pandemic and undertaken in addition to the usual annual employee engagement survey, findings indicated that some people were still faced with IT challenges while working from home, and equipment may not have been suitable for long-term working. So, in August 2020 we launched our Standard Home Office Equipment (SHOE) project. The project engaged with:

- Our Safety, Health and Environment colleagues to create the Display Screen Equipment (DSE) specific IT bundles available to order.
- Senior Managers and Directors to identify and provide their people working from home with supplementary IT equipment to improve their home office set up, centrally funded by the business
- Digital and Technology teams worked together to develop solutions for staff who had technical problems working from home.

Nearly 4500 colleagues responded, indicating that they had a requirement and there were over 6000 deliveries of equipment enabling colleagues to work more effectively and healthily from home.

Clear guidance provided by employers will help clarify when in-person interactions would be most effective, and therefore recommended. The following example, again from Transport for London, in the early stages of the pandemic highlights the value of communicating clear guidance.

Transport for London – Choice with Guidance. A balanced approach.

Dr Samantha Philips – Head of Health and Wellbeing, TfL

Providing employees with choice with guidance on the purpose of the office environment ensures transparency on expectations from the business and trust through employee autonomy on deciding where to work.

In response to the pandemic TfL set up a New Ways of Working group involving representatives from across the business, including experts in health and safety, facilities, HR, comms etc to consider the implications of the pandemic on future ways of working.

The group gained feedback from across the business to shape and form the plans and announced a plan to move to hybrid ways of working. To test the success, a transition phase starting in August 2021 was planned. For the first three months colleagues attended the workplace for a couple of days a week on a voluntary basis. This then became a regular expectation.

The plan was underpinned by a number of guiding principles and the 5 Cs. Office-based working will enable the 5 Cs – cohesion, collaboration, culture, confidence and care.

Hybrid working facilitates a greater degree of agility in colleagues' working arrangements, understanding that individual circumstances and business needs will play a significant part in designing how teams will operate in their new ways of working.

The intranet site describes the journey to date and has a lot of advice and information for managers and colleagues.

HOW TO SUPPORT MANAGERS

While E-leadership can achieve the same goals as traditional leadership, through information technology (Iriqat & Khalaf, 2017), manager perceptions and experiences, indicate there are additional challenges to managing remote workers. It has been shown that being a leader when work is organised virtually is generally more difficult than leading traditional teams (Arnfalk et al., 2016) and telework requires strong leadership (Snellman, 2014). Manager training during the Covid-19 pandemic positively impacted perceived productivity. Research by the CIPD in 2021 showed that perceptions of productivity differed between those organisations that had offered line manager training in managing remote workers and those that did not. Of those employers who offered such training, 43% said productivity had increased during homeworking, compared to only 29% that had not offered training (CIPD, 2021). Equipping managers with the right skills to ensure quality communications and relationships, for example, through developing 'remote working training for managers' can help build their confidence to manage within this relatively new way of working. This could be as simple as providing a self-learning training package or holding virtual webinars.

The following example shows how Devon and Cornwall Police adapted their approach to support individuals and line managers:

Devon and Cornwall Police – New ways of working.

Professor John Harrison – Chief Medical Officer

Coming on the back of 2020, it is, perhaps, not surprising that our people are showing signs of strain. There was clear evidence of an impact on wellbeing over the year. However, we are bending but not breaking. We are now redoubling our efforts on team wellbeing, whilst reinforcing messages about individual wellbeing and resilience. New ways of working, that have been accelerated by Covid restrictions, are impacting wellbeing and our approach. We are building on the resources and initiatives we have put in place to date, and now emphasising the role of managers and leaders to address team wellbeing.

Working from home/hybrid working/spending lots of time communicating on Microsoft Teams is a challenge. It is throwing up lots of examples of healthy/unhealthy ways of working. We are all different and respond positively or negatively according to our individual circumstances. Managers are having to learn new ways to check in with their teams and understanding how best to work together.

I am pleased to report that the Force has been very sensitive to people's needs, particularly with respect to Covid anxieties and vulnerabilities. We have been slow to push returning to work on site, although that is now being pursued, with care.

Taking a tailored approach, enabled by line manager training, will ensure consideration of the needs of each individual. The following describes learnings from workplace experiments aimed at optimising the hybrid working experience for the individual and the company.

Ryan Hopkins – Future of Wellbeing Leader at Deloitte; LinkedIn Top Voice; TEDx Speaker; Author of *52 Weeks of Wellbeing*

In late 2021 Satya Nadella, the Microsoft CEO, stated that solving the hybrid paradox will be the challenge of the decade. In 2021 Microsoft surveyed more than 30,000 of its people across 31 countries, which revealed that 73% of respondents would like for the flexibility they've experienced during the pandemic and beyond to continue. At the same time, 67% say they want more in-person time with colleagues too.

It isn't just Satya who is trying to solve the hybrid paradox, I tried to unpick this puzzle at a large tech company previously – 10,000+ colleagues, 30+ different countries. It was our intention to create a place where people loved to work – enabling colleagues to work when, where and how they wanted, from hybrid work to unlimited paid vacation. We were quick out of the gates and announced that we were going hybrid in December 2020 with a 2+ policy – 2 days a week at home, 2 days a week in the office and 1 flex day for you to decide – where previously colleagues worked 4–5 days a week in the office. This flexibility was welcomed with open arms at first. Utilisation averaged between 5–25%. What would have been seen as a massively positive step 2 years prior (imagine being offered 2–3 days to work from home pre-pandemic), was actually perceived to be rather draconian. When people did come into the office, they found themselves sitting on back-to-back calls. We soon learned that there is no panacea for hybrid and one size does certainly not fit all. The desire to return to the office dropped from circa. 80% in 2020 to 36% in early 2022.

What did we learn?

What went well:

– We focused on collecting and telling colleague anecdotes in sites as they reopened and these were received very well, shifting the colleague engagement content from more professional to short-form and fun – colleague interaction with initiatives went up 110% in a year and no budget was spent on 'high quality' campaigns.
– We focused on creating space away from laptops when in the office and at home, developing the concept of digital balance – how to define digital boundaries to create space in the digital environment. I eventually spoke at Microsoft, speaking about how their tech could be used in a sustainable manner. We ran campaigns throughout the year, created world firsts – the in-office OOO (put your OOO on when you're in the office to let people know that there is a delay in your online correspondence and that you will be back in the virtual office tomorrow) over a year, we reduced the workweek span for the whole business by 4 hours.
– Developing the collective understanding that more input does not always mean more outcomes, it is one thing to be busy and another

to be productive. Flexibility had arrived and the people wanted more. We coached 1,200 managers how to create team charters – building the flexibility (temporal, geographic, modal) into ways of working. This saw teams taking more of their unlimited annual leave benefit, with no effect on productivity.

What didn't go so well:

- Although leaders asked their people to come back in, a lot of them did not follow their own advice. It was a case of do as I say, not as I do. You could see a clear correlation between those that led by example and those that did not.
- The sense of community was lacking, as people were coming into near-empty offices – voluntary attrition for colleagues with less than 2 years tenure was 3 times higher in December 2021 compared to December 2019. There was no organisational stickiness. On the flip side, we saw leavers come back at double the rate, further exemplifying the stickiness point.
- Engagement scores had steadily begun to drop across the business, with some interesting trends – colleagues that were co-located with their managers were more engaged than those who had international managers and that virtual colleagues were 7% less engaged than their office counterparts.

What did we pivot to?

Given all of these learnings, data points, research since and conversations I have and, on the subject, if I started again today this is how I would do it:

1) Define the baseline which everyone comes in for, creating that organisational stickiness, think organisation-wide events e.g. All Hands, important organisational dates e.g. Mental Health Week, volunteering, etc.
2) Work with leaders to define what each job type needs from a physical proximity perspective to their own team, cross-functional teams and the customer – considering collaboration, performance & connection – creating customised hybrid personas. This will result in innovative, connected, productive teams.

3) The goal of the personas is to solve the hybrid paradox, creating connection while providing flexibility, so long as KPIs and cohesion are not affected. Create a pull rather than a push. There may be circumstances where individuals need to come in more or less and they should discuss this with their managers, these circumstances may include:

   3.1.   Regional nuances – locational health & safety issues e.g., Covid regulations, cultural differences, office relocation or even safety at night.

   3.2.   Individual circumstances – Caring needs, mental health needs, shielding, home working environment, physical needs, new joiners (come in more) and finally managers/ leaders (who need to be more present).

4) Leaders should share their functional office day/s globally, so people know when x, y, z teams will be in and in-person activities can be planned around this.

Employees are willing to sacrifice 9% of their salary to work flexibly with regard to location. I would suggest that adding temporal flexibility to this would increase the figure even further. Imagine then if we were to level modal flexibility on top, enabling people to work in a way that suits them. We would create a truly world-class workplace for people from all demographics.

The future of work is temporally, geographically, modally agnostic. Companies that enable their people to work where, when and how they want will keep their best talent and attract the rest.

ACTIONS

Organisational level

- Develop and clearly communicate when in-person interactions would be more effective and therefore recommended or expected.
- Create reasons to come into the office, such as leadership communicating ahead when they plan to be on site, agree team days for being in the office, planning site events, business updates throughout the year and social events.

- Ensure health and wellbeing approaches and offerings are adapted to reach remote workers, for instance, leveraging technology through providing virtual wellbeing solutions.
- Provide wellbeing training for those working remotely, and for line managers, to help them understand how to support their staff to enhance their teams' experience of inclusion and wellbeing and enable them to remain productive.

Manager level

- Understand the preferences of your employees in relation to flexible working and consider, as far as possible, how to match these to business needs.
- As wellbeing is strongly liked to productivity, hold regular check-in meetings with your employees with a focus on self-care, including their work–life balance, mental, physical and emotional wellbeing, and consider how to connect remote workers with others in the team. Provide them with the tools and equipment to enable them to do their job effectively.
- Focus on outputs, rather than physical presence, in performance evaluations.

REFERENCES

Arnfalk, P., Pilerot, U., Schillander, P., & Grönvall, P. (2016). Green IT in practice: Virtual meetings in Swedish public agencies. *Journal of Cleaner Production*, 123, 101–112.

Beckers, D.G.J., Kompier, M.A.J., Kecklund, G., & Härmä, M. (2012). Worktime control: Theoretical conceptualization, current empirical knowledge, and research agenda. Scandinavian Journal of Work, *Environment and Health*, 38(4), 291–297.

Benetytė, D., & Jatuliavičienė, G. (2013). Building and sustaining trust in virtual teams within organizational context. *Regional Formation & Development Studies*, (10).

Bloom, N., Liang, J., Roberts, J., & Ying, Z.J. (2015). Does working from home work? Evidence from a Chinese experiment. *Quarterly Journal of Economics*, 130, 165–218.

Boston Consulting Group (2020). Survey shows employees felt surprisingly productive during COVID-19. Retrieved November 27, from Survey Shows Employees Felt Surprisingly Productive During COVID-19 (bcg.com).

Chawla, N., MacGowan, R.L., Gabriel, A.S., & Podsakoff, N.P. (2020). Unplugging or staying connected? Examining the nature, antecedents, and consequences of profiles of daily recovery experiences. *Journal of Applied Psychology*, 105(1), 19.

CIPD. (2021). Flexible working: Lessons from the pandemic. Retrieved from https://www.cipd.co.uk/knowledge/fundamentals/relations/flexible-working/flexible-working-lessons-pandemic

CIPD. (2023). Flexible working - the impact of COVID-19. Retrieved November 27, from https://www.cipd.co.uk/knowledge/fundamentals/relations/flexible-working/flexible-working-impact-covid#gref

Chesley, N. (2014). Information and communication technology use, work intensification and employee strain and distress. *Work, Employment and Society*, 28, 589–610.

Daim, T.U., Ha, A., Reutiman, S., Hughes, B., Pathak, U., Bynum, W., & Bhatla, A. (2012). Exploring the communication breakdown in global virtual teams. *International Journal of Project Management*, 30(2), 199–212.

Del Boca, D., Oggero, N., Profeta, P., & Rossi, M.C. (2020). Women's work, housework and childcare, before and during COVID-19. *COVID Economics: Vetted and Real-Time Papers, Issue* 28, 70–90.

Demerouti, E., Derks, D., Ten Brummelhuis, L.L., & Bakker, A.B. (2014). New ways of working: Impact on working conditions, work–family balance, and well-being. *The Impact of ICT on Quality of Working Life*, 123–141.

Global Work Analytics. (n.d.). Work from home experience survey results. Retrieved, November 27, from https://globalworkplaceanalytics.com/global-work-from-home-experience-survey

Felstead, A., & Henseke, G. (2017). Assessing the growth of remote working and its consequences for effort, well-being and work-life balance. *New Technology, Work and Employment*, 32, 195–212.

Hoeven, C., & Zoonen, W. (2015). Flexible work designs and employee well-being: Examining the effects of resources and demands. *New Technology, Work and Employment*, 30, 237–255.

Holt-Lunstad, J., Smith, T.B., Baker, M., Harris, T., & Stephenson, D. (2015). Loneliness and social isolation as risk factors for mortality: A meta-analytic review. *Perspectives on Psychological Science*, 10(2), 227–237.

International Monetary Fund (2020). *World economic outlook, October 2020: A Long and Difficult Ascent*. https://www.imf.org/en/Publications/WEO/Issues/2020/09/30/world-economic-outlook-october-2020

Iriqat, R.A.M., & Khalaf, D.M.S. (2017). Using e-leadership as a strategic tool in enhancing organizational commitment of virtual teams in foreign commercial banks in North West Bank - Palestine. *International Journal of Business Administration*, 8(7), 25–32.

Kappel, S., Schmitt, O., Finnegan, E., & Fureix, C. (2021). Learning from lockdown - Assessing the positive and negative experiences, and coping strategies of researchers during the COVID-19 pandemic. *Applied Animal Behaviour Science*, 236, 105269.

Kelliher, C., & Anderson, D. (2010). Doing more with less? Flexible working practices and the intensification of work. *Human Relations*, 63, 83–106.

Kopp, R.E. (2020). Loneliness in the age of COVID-19. *Psychology & Marketing*, 37(8), 987–994.

Kotera, Y., Green, P., & Sheffield, D. (2020). Work-life balance of UK construction workers: Relationship with mental health. *Construction Management and Economics*, 38(3), 291–303.

Lai, J., Ma, S., Wang, Y., et al. (2020). Factors associated with mental health outcomes among health care workers exposed to coronavirus disease 2019. *JAMA Netw Open*, 3(3), e203976.

Mazmanian, M., Orlikowski, W.J., & Yates, J.A. (2013). The autonomy paradox: The implications of mobile email devices for knowledge professionals. *Organization Science*, 24(5), 1337–1357.

Miller, A.M. (2020). People who got sick with the coronavirus while living alone describe their panic: 'I could be dead and decaying and no one would know'. https://www.businessinsider.com/what-its-like-to-get-covid-19-when-living-alone-2020-5

Moen, P., Kelly, E.L., & Hill, R. (2011). Does enhancing work-time control and flexibility reduce turnover? A naturally occurring experiment. *Social Problems*, 58(1), 69–98.

Mogale, L., & Sutherland, M. (2010). Managing virtual teams in multinational companies. *South African Journal of Labour Relations*, 34, 7–24.

Morganson, V.J., Major, D.A., Oborn, K.L., Verive, J.M., & Heelan, M.P., (2010). Comparing telework locations and traditional work arrangements: Differences in work-life balance support, job satisfaction, and inclusion. *Journal of Managerial Psychology*, 25(6), 578–595.

Nitschke, J.P., Forbes, P.A., Ali, N., Cutler, J., Apps, M.A., Lockwood, P.L., & Lamm, C. (2021). Resilience during uncertainty? Greater social connectedness during COVID-19 lockdown is associated with reduced distress and fatigue. *British Journal of Health Psychology*, 26(2), 553–569.

Norris-Green, M., & Gifford, J. (2021). *CIPD good work index 2021*. London: Chartered Institute of Personnel and Development.

Pritchard, R.D., & Payne, S.C. (2003). Performance management practices and motivation. *The new workplace: People, technology and organisation: A handbook and guide to the human impact of modern working practices* (pp. 219–244). New York: John Wiley.

Raišienė, A.G., Rapuano, V., Varkulevičiūtė, K., & Stachová, K., (2020). Working from home—Who is happy? A survey of Lithuania's employees during the COVID-19 quarantine period. *Sustainability*, 12, 5332.

Raheel, M. (2014). Relationship between loneliness, psychiatric disorders and physical health? A review on the psychological aspects of loneliness. *Journal of Clinical and Diagnostic Research*, 8(9), 320–322.

Robinson, A. (2020). Loneliness in the age of COVID-19. *Psychology & Marketing*, 37(8), 987–994.

Russo, D., Hanel, P.H., Altnickel, S., & van Berkel, N., (2021). Predictors of well-being and productivity among software professionals during the COVID-19 pandemic–A longitudinal study. *Empirical Software Engineering*, 26(4), 62.

Smith, R.A. (2020). Single life and the coronavirus. https://www.wsj.com/articles/single-life-and-the-coronavirus-11586088001.

Snellman, C.L. (2014). Virtual teams: Opportunities and challenges for e-Leaders. *Procedia—Social and Behavioral Sciences*, 110, 1251–1261.

Sonnentag, S. (2012). Psychological detachment from work during leisure time: The benefits of mentally disengaging from work. *Current Directions in Psychological Science*, 21(2), 114–118.

Tiwari, S.C. (2013). Loneliness: A disease? *Indian Journal of Psychiatry*, 55(4), 320.

Van Steenbergen, E.F., van der Ven, C., Peeters, M.C.W., & Taris, T.W., (2018). Transitioning towards new ways of working: Do job demands, job resources, burnout, and engagement change? *Psychological Reports*, 121(4), 736–766.

Wang, J., Mann, F., Lloyd-Evans, B., Ma, R., & Johnson, S., (2018). Associations between loneliness and perceived social support and outcomes of mental health problems: A systematic review. *BMC Psychiatry*, 18(1), 1–16.

Walton, S., O'Kane, P., & Ruwhiu, D. (2020). *New Zealanders' attitudes towards working from home*. Technical Report, University of Otago.

Wolor, C., Solikhah, N., & Fadillah, N. (2020). Effectiveness of e-training, e-leadership, and work life balance on employee performance during COVID-19. *Journal of Asian Finance Economics and Business*, 7, 443–450.

THE FIVE FUNDAMENTALS OF SUCCESS

Key messages

1. Data must guide all decision-making, from identifying health and wellbeing needs, to setting the strategy, to regularly reviewing the impact of investments made. For instance, which employee groups to target, which solutions to invest in and whether to continue providing existing offerings or seek alternatives.

2. Be inclusive in your approach to EH&W. This means seeking employee views on what they need to enhance their wellbeing and how they would prefer to access solutions, gaining feedback on proposed solutions and leveraging employee passion to become EH&W ambassadors and champions. Respect cultural differences when promoting and communicating wellbeing and ensure an approach that is personalised and therefore relevant, and also flexible, to meet the changing needs of employees.

3. Harnessing employee passion to support each other, such as through peer-to-peer health and wellbeing support networks, can be motivating and rewarding for the support giver, and highly valued by colleagues at the receiving end. Training and supervision must be made compulsory, to support a consistent approach, to provide clarity on expectations and to enable debriefing, for those offering this service

4. Leveraging technology and integrating EH&W efforts with key business partners that have a stake in EH&W will enhance employee reach and awareness, and thereby impact.

5. Sourcing occupational health and wellbeing expertise ensures that a data-driven, evidence-based, strategic and comprehensive approach is taken.

DOI: 10.4324/9781003124979-6

> 6. Regularly reviewing the impact of interventions, through seeking quantitative and qualitative data, and using this to adapt approach accordingly, will ensure solutions continue to match greatest needs.

THE FIVE FUNDAMENTALS

There is, rather promisingly, an upward trend in investment in employee health and wellbeing within organisations, driven by well-intentioned leaders. While this is a positive step, there are key considerations that should form the basis of every wellbeing approach. Applying these fundamental success factors will ensure maximal benefit for employees and organisational impact from these investments. While implementing all five may not be possible immediately,

Figure 6.1 The fundamentals to implementing an effective health and wellbeing strategy

using them as a guide when considering how to evolve your EH&W approach, might be helpful.

These factors provide a guide for approaching EH&W, from diagnosis, to design, to implementation and subsequently reviewing approach.

1. **Data-driven decisions**
2. **Inclusive approach**
3. **Health and wellbeing expertise**
4. **Expand awareness and access**
5. **Measure impact and act**.

1. Data-driven decision-making

Leading with a data-driven approach ensures all decisions are well informed, with clear rationale. Ways in which data can help include measuring employee health status, gaining employee insights, identifying correlations between EH&W and business interests, identifying which solutions to provide and measuring their impact. There are many examples within workplaces, where health and wellbeing services have been implemented without assessing whether or not there was a need for them. Without any significant need, uptake and value from any investment will be poor. With increasing access today, to anonymised and aggregate employee data, such as health behaviours and the status of wellbeing of employees, organisations can gain valuable insights into where the greatest needs are, and are now, more than ever, well placed to provide the most relevant solutions.

Readily available or bespoke digital tools can help identify employee wellbeing needs, such as apps and wearables. The following example from John Lewis shows how the results from health screening initiatives informed the company where employees needed the most wellbeing support. This was used to identify solutions and inform and improve their recruitment process.

John Lewis – Night Shift Workers' Sleep Intervention.

Nick Davison – former Head of Health and Wellbeing

The analysis of a routine health screening initiative within John Lewis Partnership's distribution network identified that 45% of responding

Partners (employees) were self-reporting an average of less than seven hours' sleep per day. The supply chain is critical to the management of stock from suppliers, the replenishment of shops and plays a central role in online sales fulfilment.

Partners' use of a positive psychology and educational digital tool reinforced the need for great exploration and education with 'tiredness' consistently reported as the most common sentiment by Partners at initial "check-in".

In response, the Partnership began a new collaborative project called the 'Night Club'. This combined in-house clinicians, supply chain nightshift operational stakeholders, a third-party and external expertise from Wellcome Trust and Oxford University's Sleep and Circadian Neuroscience Institute. The objective was to help night-shift Partners improve the quality of their sleep within the context of shift work and their work environment.

Set within a shipping container, the project toured distribution centres, providing nightshift Partners with an opportunity to speak directly with nutritionists, sleep specialists and the Partnership's own Occupational Health Advisors. Those attending had the opportunity to try healthy food and drinks and new technologies to aid sleep such as wearing 'Re-timer Light Therapy goggles' and the use of medical-grade SAD lamps. In addition, they learned about their specific 'chronotype' by completing a simple Chronotyping Questionnaire.

In total, 535 night-shift workers took part, with 65% saying they would change what they do to improve their sleep as a result of the project. The Chronotyping Questionnaire revealed that partners broadly fell into categories seen in the general population with 25% 'extreme night owls', 25% 'extreme larks' and 50% somewhere 'in between'. The results were shared with the recruitment team in order to consider how chronotype preferences could operate within the recruitment strategy.

EH&W needs can be identified through a variety of sources, for instance, aggregate employee health and wellbeing data (such as data from health screening or through use of wearables or Apps), company culture and manager surveys, insights gained from employee focus group interviews and Employee Resource Groups (ERGs). Once these needs have been identified, it is critical that any solutions considered are evidence based.

Data must also be sought to review the impact of initiatives, which will help inform whether they are successful or a different approach, such as investing in raising awareness of the services, or even whether to explore alternative services if impact is less than desirable. Deciding to stop less valuable services is not a common practice in the workplace. This is possibly a result of insufficient thought given, at the planning stage of implementing a service to goals and targets or even a commitment to review effectiveness.

2. Inclusive approach

Providing a service without closely consulting with the customer for whom the service is intended, such as seeking input and feedback, seems illogical. However, this is unfortunately a common reality. Feedback is a critical data source. Being inclusive entails leveraging the passion of your employee population. Employees offer valuable perspectives, insights and personal resources. There are many examples of how this is done extremely well within organisations. Ways in which they can get involved include sharing their employee health and wellbeing needs and personal stories, co-creating solutions, helping to successfully launch and embed them, offering feedback on existing resources, promoting wellbeing and supporting each other.

a) Seek voice of the customer

Using knowledgeable and experienced expertise to identify evidence-based solutions provides credibility and rigour; however, expertise alone will not guarantee success. Sufficient input from end users, for whom these solutions are provided, will ensure needs are met, and utilisation and impact maximised.

Research has identified that healthcare professionals requested five things from their employer during the Covid-19 pandemic: hear me, protect me, prepare me, support me, and care for me (Shanafelt et al., 2020). By understanding employee needs, organisations can work towards addressing them, resulting in employees feeling valued, motivated and engaged. In a UK healthcare worker study (Blake et al., 2020), the authors found that online materials needed to go beyond the generic promotion of health and must address issues that were *specifically* relevant, in this instance, to healthcare workplace environments (e.g., shift work), as well as specific issues experienced by healthcare workers during Covid-19 (e.g., dealing with difficult decisions and coping with guilt during self-isolation).

The NHS check study demonstrated the value of seeking the voice of the customer (Lamb et al., 2021). This study shed light on what employees value, and emphasised the importance of seeking employee opinion and evaluating the uptake of resources on offer. The support services used, and therefore presumably most useful, were staff discounts, general online resources and free wellbeing apps. However, rather surprisingly, the least used services (7% or less) were staff support lines i.e., the counselling service, also known as Employee Assistance Program (EAP), a mental health support service that is commonplace within many organisations. This raises the question of whether EH&W services in place within organisations are deemed useful by the people for whom they are sourced, and highlights the importance of measuring the utilisation of existing services, together with seeking feedback on the value of such services. In today's world, where investment and impact are heavily scrutinised, ensuring maximal value from investments made is critical.

The development stage of potential health and wellbeing solutions must consider employee opinion. The following example, from SUEZ recycling and recovery UK, exemplifies the impact that employee involvement can have on the success of wellbeing efforts.

SUEZ recycling and recovery UK – Involving employees from the outset.

Dr Tracey Leghorn – Chief Business Services Officer and Natalie Sáenz – SW Regional Communications Manager

Our Wellness for All programme is now in its third year and it's important to remember that the success of our wellbeing support programme has always been about employee engagement. Wellness for

All was designed for our people, by our people and it continues to be shaped by responding to the evolving needs of our employees.

In autumn 2019, led by our Chief Business Services Officer, Dr Tracey Leghorn, our Works Council and over 50 of our employees came together and developed our 'Wellness Charter' with a vision of 'Wellness for All'. These enshrined what wellbeing meant to them and how the company could best support everyone to thrive and be their authentic selves.

b) Use employee passion to promote wellbeing (Ambassadors/ Champions/Employee Resource groups)

Health and wellbeing champions, and ambassadors, are employees who, as a result of their passion in health and wellbeing, offer to promote available wellbeing resources to other employees, in addition to their day job. This can be one of the most powerful ways to reach employees. SUEZ recycling and recovery UK, introduced an ambassador network, with tangible benefits.

SUEZ recycling and recovery UK.

Dr Tracey Leghorn – Chief Business Services Officer and Natalie Sáenz – SW Regional Communications Manager

Engagement amongst frontline employees was slow to begin with, so we decided to introduce Regional Wellbeing and Inclusion Ambassadors to bring the programme closer to the ground. All of our initial 12 ambassadors across the UK were volunteers. They are operationally based, so they are familiar with the culture and the work environment and they can help support Health and Wellbeing campaigns and drive engagement with our frontline workers. To prepare them for their role they have undergone a training programme which includes a Level 3 First Aid for Mental Health course, Domestic Abuse training with Women's Aid and a 6-week wellbeing course with our wellbeing external partner. They meet bi-monthly with our Wellbeing and Inclusion Manager to help shape the Wellness for All programme and support wellbeing campaigns. In 2023, this increased to 20 volunteer ambassadors (each provided with a half-day's protected time a week), strategically located to cover all 300 of our sites across the UK along with two fulltime Wellbeing and Inclusion Officers, who were dedicated to supporting and coordinating our ambassadors and working closely with Regional Managers and HR Officers to provide effective support where needed.

Within the first two months of our Wellbeing and Inclusion Ambassadors being in place we saw a huge increase in engagement with our Wellness for All programme, including a 14% increase in registration for our Employee Assistance Programme, WeCare. Some of our operational sites have organised wellbeing coffee mornings, for example, where awareness information is shared on a number of wellbeing topics and wellbeing conversations take place. Other sites have organised wellbeing areas where information and support can be found, and they have become 'go to' places for '5 minutes of time-out' during a busy day.

We communicated the launch of our ambassadors through our quarterly *Suez Life* magazine that's posted to all employees, the monthly Health, Safety and Wellbeing newsletter and posters displayed at sites with contact details of their local ambassador.

It is relatively easy to set up ambassador or champion groups and provide them with support, through training and supervision from health and wellbeing experts. Employee Resource groups (ERGs) are another influential group. SUEZ recycling and recovery UK leverages their various ERGs to raise awareness of health and wellbeing resources, and introduce policies, processes and solutions to better support the wellbeing of their employees. As the health and wellbeing of employees intersects all ERGs, promoting EH&W resources is universally relevant.

Our Inclusion and Diversity Networks provide a safe space to discuss any challenges and to work on projects that have a positive impact on our people. This year our LGBTQIA+ Network has worked on raising awareness and educating colleagues, the Disabilities group has worked on an adjustment passport to support colleagues as they move around the business in different roles, the Multicultural group has created mentoring opportunities and our Women's Network has driven change in some of our HR policies and introduced workwear for women at SUEZ.

British Telecom has an extensive champion network in place:

British Telecom – Wellbeing Champions.

Richard Caddis – Chief Medical Officer

This was launched in January 2021, as a separate initiative from the already existing employee peer-to-peer (mental health first aid) network. The BT wellbeing champions network has over 500 champions located around the globe. The wellbeing champions are all trained volunteers who have received an induction training into the role. The governance is overseen from the centre with a rolling quarterly programme of additional training aligned to the group wellbeing strategy. All of the wellbeing champions are aligned to one of BT's main divisions and also take part in their divisionally led initiatives.

c) Offer and encourage peer-to-peer support (with oversight)

It is easy to understand why employees are more likely to talk to each other about their challenges than they are to their manager. As a result, peer-to-peer support is gaining momentum across organisations, with many employees keen to support their colleagues. Peer support involves making oneself available to listen to colleagues as and when they would like to talk, and signposting them to supportive resources. Two principles must accompany this initiative. Those who volunteer need to be trained on how they can help their colleagues to ensure consistency, quality and clarity of roles and responsibilities. They should also have some degree of supervision, to enable them to maintain boundaries, continue to learn and have a safe space to debrief.

The following example at BAM, UK and IRL. shows how wellbeing, within a civil engineering and construction company, was overseen by experts but driven by their people, for their people.

BAM UK& IRL – Impact of the Wellbeing Champion. BAM.

Rhianwen Condron – Wellbeing Lead, BAM

BAM UK&IRL is a civil engineering and construction company, with around 6500 employees and sites and projects across the UK and Ireland. They are part of the Royal BAM Group, based in the Netherlands with a total headcount around 18,000 employees.

Our evolution of the site-based wellbeing agenda was kickstarted when a project director (business leader) with a great interest in wellbeing asked me to set up and manage the original Wellbeing Room. Prior to this we had done a lot of work on this project with our site teams about mental health and wellbeing. This included such things as Wellbeing Champions (trained mental health first aiders) in site compounds at set times and days each week, available to talk about any issues. Some Wellbeing Champions also carried out site tours weekly, asking people how they were, and what was going on in their lives. We developed a monthly wellbeing plan which included initiatives such as arranging for a podiatrist to visit site monthly (staff members were wearing boots and walking 10+ miles daily), smoothie bikes, and meditation and mindfulness sessions. The Wellbeing Room seemed to be a natural forward step from this.

The rooms are staffed by Wellbeing Champions. At times when it is impossible to have someone in the room, the rooms are open to provide an area for people to go and have a quiet time in. There are posters on the walls with contact details for wellbeing champions, as well as EAP and charity phone numbers and posters.

The key to the success of the wellbeing rooms has been people coming in to talk to someone, and then going back out on site and recommending the room/service to others. Our site teams spend a lot of time with their colleagues, and I've found that they are very good at picking up when someone is not their usual self. Recommendation brings so many people in. Trust in the people staffing the room is key, and I think the fact that these rooms don't look or feel like work. Our site supervisors are more than happy for members of their teams to come in and use the facilities and the whole project teams are fully behind the concept of the wellbeing rooms. These rooms give a private, confidential space for people to come in and talk. These conversations included the following: the rape of a family member, suicide, lack of intimacy with partners (which often leads to conversations on the menopause), a lack of self-belief, the impact of drugs, alcohol, and gambling, the loss of sex drive, and historic sexual abuse (of one employee by another).

We have a number of testimonials. The impact on people willing to talk has been massive: on our Time to Talk webinar in 2022, we had two individuals who wanted to share their stories. One was a traditional big and burly man who had never talked about his emotions but shared the value of doing this with a counsellor through work and the amazing support that was available to him though the wellbeing team to help him recover. The other was a gambler, an alcoholic who wanted to share his story of the power of opening up to a champion and how much support they gave him. The impact of both (and others) has been massive and is really bringing other people forward to open up and share and get the support they need.

British Telecom has well-established peer-to-peer mental health first aiders, as well as wellbeing champions:

British Telecom – Peer2 Peer Mental Health First Aider.

Richard Caddis – Chief Medical Officer

Formerly launched in 2017 as one of BT's Employee Networks specifically to help colleagues with mental health issues, the network has rapidly grown to over 1200 members in the following countries: the United Kingdom, the United States, India, China, Ireland, Brazil, the United Arab Emirates, Hungary, Mexico, Singapore, South Africa, Australia, Hong Kong, Japan, Malaysia, Canada, Chile, Belgium, Argentina, Costa Rica, Colombia, Italy, Netherlands, South Korea, and Thailand. The network has over 400 trained volunteers in mental health first aid. There is a rigorous process to become a trained volunteer. In addition to mental health training, the volunteers have to be deemed to be suitable by their line manager and have an external reference. Before they actually start, they also have specific induction training and sign a charter (a code of conduct). Once they have completed this process and commenced in the role, they receive a lot of support. There is a core team of experienced peer-to-peer volunteers always available, and ongoing training provided at least quarterly. The volunteers can refer and talk through specific cases with the EAP, and they also have access to a psychotherapist.

The following example, from the UK NHS, shows the value of peer support (for those working in highly stressful environments, where traumatic events are not uncommonly experienced), and the resulting impact on individuals and the organisation. It also emphasises the importance of high-quality, evidence-based training and supervision.

Wrightington Wigan and Leigh Teaching Hospitals NHS Foundation Trust. Peer support for critical incidents – Critical Incident Stress Management (CISM) Service.

Zoe Garnett – Staff Wellbeing Manager

As an NHS Acute Hospital Trust, we had a specific need to support the wellbeing of our staff after traumatic events. We found that staff were having to deal with these events without there being any formal immediate support in place, other than general colleague/management social support. We were seeing a trend in staff sickness and wellbeing data, where some events had proved too much for some staff members to cope with. We did not have the appropriate immediate aftercare in place to support staff after critical events, and we felt that not only did we have a duty of care to provide that support, but it might actually have a beneficial impact on staff wellbeing, sickness and performance.

The approach we use is accredited by the International Critical Incident Stress Foundation (ICISF) and the University of Maryland.

A cohort of 17 staff members were trained initially by an organisation with over 40 years' experience of working with trauma and delivering the types of interventions that would enable us to better support staff wellbeing. This was done via a number of face-to-face training days where attendees had the opportunity to learn the theory and practice their skills before being signed off as competent to practice with our CISM team.

To support the wellbeing of our CISM team, there are a number of factors in place such as:

- CISM interventions should always be facilitated in pairs, not alone.
- CISM debriefers are required to have a debrief between themselves afterwards to check in with each other. They can also call a member of the Steps4Wellness team for a debrief if it has been a particularly tough topic to process.
- All CISM debriefers are able to say "No" to facilitating a debrief at any time if they feel they will be putting their own wellbeing at risk by doing so – for example, if the topic of the debrief may trigger a past event for them.
- Quarterly CPD events are offered to debriefers for continued development in the role and to allow the CISM leads to re-assess competence.
- The CISM leads meet monthly to discuss and review the CISM triage forms that have been submitted and the decisions made as to which intervention was most appropriate.

Since the pandemic entered the recovery phase, we have reviewed our psychological first aid service including a rebrand of the offer now known as 'Supporting People After Critical Events (SPACE)'. This includes CISM as a group intervention and Trauma Risk Management (TRiM) as an individual support option.

TRiM is a focused peer support system which aims to support people who have experienced a traumatic, or potentially traumatic, incident. Essentially, by using a screening tool, staff can undertake an assessment which helps to identify individuals early on who may be at risk of experiencing a delay in their recovery from the incident, and builds resilience through the provision of support and education to these individuals or referral on to other professional teams/services.

Whilst CISM is strongly indicated and effective as a group crisis intervention and will continue to be needed on occasions across the organisation, following pandemic recovery, there was an increasing need to provide trauma support in a different way on a more individual basis. Critical events can affect staff in different ways and individual support may be more appropriate at times than group crisis intervention, as had become evident recently in the number of requests for such individualised support received by the Steps4Wellness Team. A more sustainable and fit-for-purpose solution for future provision of psychological first aid was required at WWL and TRiM was the chosen evidence-based solution.

We trained 40 TRiM Practitioners in July 2023 and had 13 incidents referred to the TRiM service in the first 4 months since its introduction. We have reached out to over 50 staff members involved in these incidents to offer TRiM assessments and also to provide psycho-education as to the 'normal' impacts they may experience as a result of exposure to such incidents.

As with the CISM team, we provide wellbeing support to our TRiM Practitioners in similar ways, i.e. options to debrief, to opt out for periods of time or particular incidents, facilitation of CPD events.

d) Consider the cultural dimension

While it may be more convenient to take a 'one size fits all' approach to wellbeing, culture plays a big role in how we view and discuss wellbeing and the degree to which we engage in any available wellbeing initiative. Exploring cultural differences in how initiatives land will enable a tailored approach that is both sensitive and effective. For instance, in the UK, promoting and talking about the menopause, within the workplace, is gaining traction. Interventions such as educating employees on the menopause and how it can impact those that are experiencing symptoms of menopause, and providing manager training on how to have discussions with employees can better support our female population. While these interventions may be acceptable within certain cultures, they may not be in others. Geography also plays a role. For instance, mental health may be easier to discuss with employees in the US, where it is more socially acceptable to talk about mental health challenges, than it would be in Southeast Asia, where stigma is more prevalent, and where therefore, there may be a reluctance to open up and talk about it. Providing employees and managers with such awareness, as part of inclusion and leadership training for instance, can help them adapt their approach. Culture must also be considered when measuring wellbeing data. Reporting on the uptake of and the setting of goals around the usage of wellbeing services, such as the employee counselling service(EAP), may be a useful indicator of perceived value where it is culturally acceptable to use this service, but less so where stigma is such that it hinders uptake. In which case, investing instead in an alternative and more acceptable solution should be considered. Interpreting company survey results also requires an understanding of cultural nuances. For example, UK employees may be more likely to indicate how they feel when completing a company survey, compared to employees in China or India, for instance, where this is not commonplace, and may give rise to false reassurances.

e) Offer personalised solutions that are flexible

The pandemic emphasised the need to adapt, quickly, to provide the most impactful services, that addressed the changing needs of staff. The following example, from UK Policing, shows how their personalised and flexible approach to wellbeing enhanced employee culture in a measurable way.

UK Policing.

Andy Rhodes – former Chief Constable, Lancashire Police UK. Service Director National Police Wellbeing Service. – Oscar Kilo. Dr Ian Hesketh – Wellbeing Lead, UK College of Policing. Senior Responsible Owner, National Police Wellbeing Service, UK Policing

The workplace should and can be a place of vital support and although remote working has been invaluable for many, we have to take a personalised view. Not everyone has the right home environment for this and not everyone feels comfortable working remotely. We have evidence that suggests our frontline have done okay in Covid-19 and yet they are the ones unable to remotely work, because social support is such an integral part of health and wellbeing. In contrast, many police office staff have heightened anxiety returning to the workplace. This is perhaps because they have not been as involved in the communications and support systems present during the height of the pandemic.

The UK police have continued to recruit on target using M365, and even our response teams (frontline officers) have done some training remotely. We have adopted and indeed accelerated technical solutions during the restrictions. Actions, such as taking statements and virtual courts, are a good example. Initially, key workers felt very anxious. However, a far more personalised and flexible approach has been taken because of things like school closures, social isolation and vulnerable persons. We propose that this is the reason why *'feeling valued by my organisation'* has improved over Covid-19.

3. Invest in workplace experts to take an evidence-based approach

Using appropriately skilled experts will pay dividends, ensuring focus is on addressing the right problems, with a data-driven, evidence-based and relevant approach that has maximal value for employees and the business. This will enable the business not just to survive, but to thrive. Expertise should be sought in the areas of occupational health, public health, strategy setting, data research and communications.

The value of occupational health expertise

The pandemic emphasised the value of occupational health professionals in supporting organisations to keep their employees safe and healthy, and ultimately ensuring business continuity. The following outlines how NHS Occupational Health service professionals played a critical role in supporting NHS employees and NHS trusts and continue to do so.

National Health Service, UK.

Dr Anne De Bono. Consultant Occupational Physician, University Hospitals of Leicester NHS Trust. Immediate Past President Faculty of Occupational Medicine

Occupational Health recognises the two-way relationship between health and work. In any industry the health of individual workers and workforce teams impacts on performance; conversely work tasks, and the circumstances in which they are carried out, impact upon workers' health. Beyond this lies a bigger picture – what happens at work also affects the wider population, nowhere more so than in the NHS. Effective safe healthcare for the population of UK plc depends upon the delivery by NHS staff of quality assessment, care and treatment.

Covid-19 Occupational Health and the NHS: *'The thin line protecting the front line.'*

An unprecedented global emergency has challenged us all, particularly NHS staff who have been at the forefront of patient care during successive waves of Covid infection and have also delivered testing and vaccination programmes. Since March 2020, much has been broadcast about them and *'Protect our NHS'* has become a national slogan, but there has been little publicity, away from specialist journals, about the support provided by Occupational Health (OH) to the largest single employer in the UK and its 1.6 million staff.

The OH contribution

Throughout the pandemic OH has provided strategic, organisational support and input to NHS decision-making at a national and local level, alongside confidential consultations and advice for clinical, administrative and support staff. OH advice has been a factor in enabling the NHS, as far as reasonably practicable, to reduce risks, establish safe systems of work, and support staff health and wellbeing to retain workability. This has, in turn, benefitted the business of healthcare, the NHS workforce and, ultimately, the patients.

On 11 March 2020 the World Health Organization declared a global pandemic and, coincidentally, the first national information and guidance document for OH services in the UK, *COVID-19 and OH in the NHS* was published. A group of NHS occupational physicians working across the UK had recognised the imminence of the Covid-19 threat, anticipated pressures on the NHS and worked at pace to review the limited available evidence about the new virus alongside established principles of OH practice. Their timely summary, before the UK's first lockdown, set a baseline for a coordinated OH response to the Covid threat, including measures to protect healthcare workers and their patients. They emphasised the importance of OH as part of strategic planning and predicted and identified key issues as:

- Risk assessment, particularly of clinical work placements.
- Management of staff who have concerns about specific vulnerability.
- Return to work after testing, isolation or illness.
- Deployment of temporary and returning staff.
- Communication.
- (In hope at that time) Vaccination.

A series of guidance documents has followed, all clinically led by groups of OH consultants from the NHS and other industries, often working in collaboration with clinicians in other disciplines. They have addressed emerging OH issues throughout the pandemic, including testing, vaccination, ethics, ethnicity, pregnancy, individual vulnerabilities and Long-Covid19, supplementing national Public Health England (PHE) and UK Health Security Agency (UKHSA) guidance to which OH consultants have also contributed.

As a result of these collaborations local NHS OH specialists and their teams have been able to access a rich seam of evidence-based information and good practice guidance over the past two years which has contributed to consistent OH advice to the NHS on a national, strategic basis, locally to NHS hospitals, community services and primary care and to individual NHS staff working throughout the UK.

The oversight of Occupational Health and wellbeing services by an experienced Occupational Health professional, who deeply understands the business in addition to the occupational health discipline, is an investment worth making. One such professional is the

'Chief Medical Officer'. While this role has existed within organisations for decades, the benefits of having a 'Chief Medical Officer' were particularly visible during the pandemic. How this role adds value to an organisation is outlined below, by Dr Paul Litchfield.

The value of a Chief Medical Officer.

Dr Paul Litchfield – Independent Chief Medical Adviser to ITV PLC & Compass Group and former Chief Medical Officer for BT Group. Visiting Professor to Coventry University

The pandemic has accelerated many trends in business and one of those is the increasing tendency to recruit a Chief Medical Officer (CMO) or Chief Health Officer (CHO). The underlying sentiment is to improve the health and wellbeing of the workforce by appointing someone who better understands health and its interface with work. The sentiment is laudable, and the action can help to deliver better business performance, but only if the person recruited has the necessary capabilities, which include relevant training and experience.

The world of healthcare is a complex and mysterious place populated by a myriad of different practitioners each with their own qualifications, professional bodies and regulators. Making sense of that and choosing the right sort of health professional can be daunting. A good starting point is to have clarity about what your business needs and what you're trying to achieve. In general, constructing an effective strategic framework for an organisation needs input from someone who has a broad understanding of health (which is more than just illness) and insight into how businesses operate. Specialists with a narrow focus (e.g., infectious disease or mental health) may be invaluable in some circumstances but are rarely well placed to take a holistic view of workforce health. Generalists, who span the full range of health issues in their training and practice, are more likely to cover all the bases and provide the comprehensive view required at a strategic level.

Many doctors and nurses, but few other health professionals, have that broad experience and they are also subject to the oversight of effective regulators who require continuing professional development supplemented by periodic appraisal to ensure standards are maintained. Much rarer are those doctors and nurses with professional training and qualifications in the two-way interaction between health and work. Training and qualifications in this discipline are most advanced in occupational medicine, though occupational health nursing is making good progress in defining standards. The UK body responsible for training and accrediting doctors in this area is the Faculty of Occupational Medicine and anyone aspiring to hold a CMO role should be qualified to Membership (MFOM) or the more experienced Fellowship (FFOM) level.

Suitable and sufficient training coupled with ongoing regulation provides considerable reassurance to a potential employer, but relevant experience is also critical. There is a tendency for companies to recruit from within their own sector but that can be unduly limiting when seeking the rare skills required to be an effective CMO or CHO. Some sectors, such as the nuclear industry, have significant health hazards to manage which do require very deep specialist knowledge but, in most cases the drivers of good and bad health are less specific. Perhaps more relevant is experience of working within a corporate environment and understanding how to navigate within an organisational structure in order to influence and stimulate change. In that respect the greatest differences are between the public and private sectors – many occupational physicians have made that transition successfully, but it has generally involved a steep learning curve at the outset.

Having narrowed a field down on the basis of qualifications and experience, it is approach and personal qualities that invariably determine the success or otherwise of an appointment. Occupational health is a science and, wherever possible, advice should be based on appropriate evidence. Professional training as an occupational physician includes the development of the skills required to assess the quality and robustness of published evidence. It also provides instruction and practice in evaluating interventions that are applied within an organisation so it can be determined whether they represent a reasonable return on investment. Most occupational physicians embed this discipline into their everyday practice, but the selection process should test whether that is, in fact, the case.

Successful CMOs are not just impersonal scientists – they also embody the qualities of a caring physician. The role requires impartiality, making decisions without fear or favour. Trust is of paramount importance and that is founded on inviolable professional confidentiality – a CMO may well be the only person in an organisation with whom key executives can share their doubts, concerns and deepest emotions. An open and non-judgemental attitude is essential with a style that favours listening over talking. Being authoritative without being dog-matic, remaining calm in a crisis and bringing gentle humour to serious conversations are all attributes that tend to be associated with per-ceived effectiveness as a CMO.

Finding the right person for this type of role in an organisation is challenging. Investing the time and trouble to achieve a good match is essential and the return for the business over years, and even decades, can be considerable.

The following case study from British Telecom highlights the value of expertise (with oversight from the Chief Medical Officer), in identifying high-risk employee population groups and taking an evidence-based approach, in this case, rehabilitation, to develop tailored health and wellbeing services for employees. This enabled workers to stay healthy, maintain their wellbeing and experience an earlier return to work.

British Telecom – rehabilitation programme for Shielders for return to the workplace.

Dr Richard Caddis – Chief Medical Officer

BT has an established history of proactively supporting colleagues with interventions such as rehabilitation physiotherapy, mental health counselling and self-service eCBT. The pandemic brought additional challenges – essentially highlighting people who became vulnerable, who may not have considered themselves vulnerable before. People who are clinically extremely vulnerable were advised to shield for an initial period of 12 weeks, always staying at home, and avoiding all face-to-face contact with others. Those with specific underlying conditions were asked by the government to "shield". We recognised this prolonged period away from work, physical activity and physical connectedness would impact on physical and mental health. Limited opportunity to maintain their usual physical activity levels could mean a decrease in physical condition and stamina to do the job as before and being worried about coming back into the workplace for a num-ber of reasons, e.g. commuting, concerns around workplace being

'Covid-secure', seeing people again, getting back in to a 'normal' routine was a common and entirely normal way to be feeling. To facilitate a safe and successful return, we have a new bespoke rehabilitation service that should be used as consideration is being given to Shielders returning to the workplace. It is intended to help people back to work by assessing their physical and psychological wellbeing and providing support should it be needed.

The Shielders programme was created for employees who have been identified by the UK government as 'clinically extremely vulnerable' and advised to shield to protect themselves from the Covid-19 virus. Line managers were expected to offer and actively encourage this new service to all of their people who had been shielding. An external provider was used to conduct the physical and psychological assessments. The level of intervention and support was informed by the severity rating and used to tailor to individual needs ranging from self-guided support through to specialised mental and physical health restoration. This informed discussions with the line manager about a phased return to work.

Using expertise to take an evidence-based approach

With the multitude of wellbeing solutions on the market, it can be overwhelming to ascertain which ones will add the greatest value. Whichever solution is chosen to address a particular wellbeing challenge, must be backed by current research. The following is an example from Serco of how health and wellbeing experts embedded interventions that had a robust evidence base. The concept of 'dual care' can be applied across other areas of wellbeing, such as mental health.

Serco – Fatigue management.

Finau Vucago – Wellbeing Manager and Kym Bancroft – Head of Health, Safety, Environment and Wellbeing, Serco

Serco AsPac takes an evidence-based approach in the development and implementation of an Advanced Fatigue Risk Management System (FRMS). The FRMS incorporates responsibility and governance, training and education, risk assessment and mitigation, and monitoring and evaluation. Within Serco AsPac the FRMS operates under a shared responsibility framework. This framework outlines a dual duty of care with regards to fatigue management.

Fatigue was identified as a risk for Serco AsPac and keen to ensure they met their duty under H&S legislation, the company wanted to ensure a safe workplace that managed fatigue risk. Anecdotal feedback and free text in the company employee survey had identified that fatigue was an emerging issue.

Fatigue management is now well embedded as one of their 13 'critical occupational safety risks' that has well-defined controls to manage the risk.

They used an evidence-based approach based on the latest research, using well-validated tools to assess sleep e.g. the Karolinska Sleepiness Scale (KSS) and a well-known fatigue expert. All tools complied with the International Organization for Standardization (ISO) standards and were legally and scientifically defensible. The ISO standard works through a risk assessment matrix that takes into account:

1. The likelihood of fatigue (based on KSS/number of hours slept in the past 24/48 hours and their shift pattern).
2. Consequences of fatigue related errors.
3. Level of risk.

Once the risk is determined, the control measures (mitigation plan) are put into place, which is determined by whether or not the individual is conducting a safety critical task. These measures are at the individual level, e.g. task rotation, having a co-driver, adding in more breaks and at the team level. The importance of *dual care* (employee and organisation) is emphasised. For instance, in the prison service, where many people work 12-hour shifts and have a commute, shared responsibility between the worker, who is encouraged to speak up and suggest how best to be supported and the employee's manager and the member of staff developing the rota to minimise fatigue risk.

Serco plans to measure the effectiveness of the fatigue programme through measuring fatigue-related incidents and fatalities and looking at cultural shifts in people feeling more able to talk about fatigue and management interest and actions to manage it through a flexible approach.

The National Institute for Health and Care Excellence (NICE) defines post-Covid syndrome, or Long Covid, as 'signs and symptoms that develop during or following an infection consistent with Covid-19 which continue for more than 12 weeks and are not explained by an alternative diagnosis' (Shah et al., 2021). Occupational health assessments, rehabilitation support, tailoring support to individual needs and promoting flexible working are ways in which companies can support individuals with Long Covid.

In this next example from British Telecom, occupational health experts developed an evidence-based rehabilitation programme for their employees with Long Covid, enabling them to feel better and return to work much sooner. This was through filling a gap in NHS service provision, to assist employees access to otherwise unavailable treatment.

British Telecom – Long Covid rehabilitation service.

Dr Richard Caddis – Chief Medical Officer, British Telecom

Those initially infected with Covid were reporting prolonged periods of ongoing symptoms, later to be called "Long Covid". With our physiotherapy service, we developed a complimentary Long Covid rehabilitation service for those who did not meet the criteria for NHS intervention. Via our professional networks, OH and rehabilitation suppliers it's believed BT were one of the first, if not the first employer of this size to create a programme to address the impact of Long Covid on our colleagues. While the NHS offered Long Covid clinics, the criteria was limited to those who had severe symptoms and were likely to need medical interventions. There were two phases: an initial self-guided intervention and a bespoke individual tailored support programme of rehabilitation.

Using evidence-based criteria at the point someone's illness would be considered long-term in nature (Long Covid) our colleagues were able to rapidly access the two-step programme.

- step 1. Guided self-help on topics such as fatigue, breathlessness, persistent cough, nutrition, mental health, activity,
- step 2. 60-minute assessment with a clinician to explore the impact on their mental and physical wellbeing, and functional capabilities

using a range of clinically validated questionnaires. Colleagues are then provided with immediate advice and support and receive ongoing 1-1 regular health coaching calls until the point of discharge. Colleagues may also be guided into other support services depending on their needs this may include our mental health service, BT Passport, workplace adjustment service.

This programme captured evidence-based approaches, NICE guidelines and published studies from the ZOE Health Study app. The input from specialist patient groups and individuals with long-term chronic conditions featured strongly in our programme architecture.

Colleagues' line managers were also provided with guidance to help them support employees to remain or return to work. As part of the programme launch our Wellbeing Leads, Wellbeing Champions and People Network Chairs were informed.

Between July 2021 and September 2022, 147 colleagues were referred to step 2 of the programme, the number of those who were off-work reduced from 46% to 12%, and those on full duties increased from 28% to 76%. Data taken from validated questionnaires also indicated a significant improvement in functional capability, wellbeing, and mental health.

Employees have provided a huge amount of positive feedback, stating that it's helped them to better understand and manage their mental and physical health and learn essential skills on pacing, managing setbacks and challenging unhelpful thoughts.

BT was honoured with a highly commended award from the British Disability Forum in 2023 for Disability Smart Inclusive Workplace Experience

4. Expand awareness and access of H&W resources

Poor uptake of available resources remains one of the biggest barriers to effectively addressing health and wellbeing challenges. This is often the result of lack of employee awareness that these services exist. A systematic approach is needed to ensure employee reach is maximised, e.g., though company-wide communications and campaigns, utilising leaders, managers, employee groups and technology to promote resources, enabling employees to pull upon these services, at their point of need.

Leverage digitalisation

During the pandemic, a McKinsey national survey of around 1000 employers found that mental health was among the top workforce health concerns, with 9 out of 10 employers surveyed noting that Covid-19 is affecting their workforce mental health and/or productivity. 77% of employers felt concerned or very concerned about mental health, 70% of employers had or planned to act, and 60% were planning to expand mental health benefits, particularly telehealth and digital tools (Coe et al., 2020). Many organisations, as a result of the pandemic, began to offer their health and wellbeing resources online. A study looking to synthesise evidence-based information, to rapidly develop and evaluate a digital learning package to support psychological wellbeing for all healthcare workers, found that within just 7 days of package release, 82% of healthcare participants reported having used the information provided in their work or home lives, and 100% anticipated they would use it in the future. It is notable that this package was very highly accessed within just 7 days of release. The package was accessed 17,633 times and had >50,000 exposures via social media within 7 days of release (Blake et al., 2020). Critical to the success of this programme was significant stakeholder feedback and peer review, in the development of the online package. While leveraging technology has helped many organisations expand reach since the pandemic, employees will only want to access support if it is relevant to their needs, engaging and easy to access. Digital content needs to be interactive and engaging. Best practices include links to external content, signposting to interactive materials such as apps, and embeding video material. It should be easy to access and flexible enough for use in different settings. Service providers, whether internal or third party in nature, need to be agile and responsive in order to adapt to the changing needs of employees.

The NHS provides apps to their staff to help them manage their wellbeing, with positive impact on symptoms and wellbeing.

NHS Wellbeing Apps.

Dr Danielle Lamb – Senior Research Fellow, University College London

One type of support being offered to staff by many NHS Trusts is access to smartphone wellbeing apps. Using the NHS CHECK cohort, a randomised controlled trial of over 1000 participants found that those using a wellbeing app ('Foundations' by Koa Health) over eight weeks had a reduction in symptoms of psychological distress and insomnia, and an improvement in wellbeing (Gnanapragasam et al., 2023).

Integrate health and wellbeing into other areas of the business

Through mapping key stakeholders who have an influence on or are impacted by the Health and Wellbeing agenda (see Chapter 2 for more on stakeholders), a more impactful and coordinated approach is possible.

SUEZ recycling and recovery UK found that linking wellbeing to their broader Health and Safety strategy and leveraging the passion of their safety teams, raised the profile of health and wellbeing and kept it on the company agenda.

SUEZ recycling and recovery UK – Integrating with Safety.

Dr Tracey Leghorn – Chief Business Services Officer and Natalie Sáenz – SW Regional Communications Manager

Positively, a 2020 employee survey showed that 81% of our employees felt that our Wellness for All programme helped to support their wellbeing and their suggestions for additional support and wellness initiative ideas were implemented. We delved deeper into the data and carried out a further survey in April 2021 with a cross-section of our, often harder to reach, frontline employees and discovered that 79% valued the wellbeing support we offered. However, we also discovered that, on average, only 48% were fully aware of the support they could access. Therefore, our focus for 2021 and 2022 was to raise awareness and engagement with Wellness for All amongst our frontline teams.

We carried out a Health and Safety survey and identified that 97% of frontline employees engaged with H&S Toolbox talks delivered by their line managers and 66% read the monthly H&S newsletter. We decided to harness our strong Health and Safety culture which had been developed through our 'Safety in Mind' behavioural change programme nearly a decade earlier. Utilising this avenue, and incorporating wellbeing into our H&S structures, policies, procedures, communications and ways of working, we have better been able to reach and engage frontline employees.

Since 2012 our award-winning Safety in Mind programme has succeeded in raising safety awareness and fostering behavioural change in an industry, which is ranked as the second most dangerous for employees in the UK. We have sought to apply some of the same lessons to proactively enhance the importance of wellbeing for our people, linking it with our broader Health and Safety strategy – prioritising the health and safety of our people beyond compliance into their holistic wellbeing as a means of enhancing their lives and performance at work.

A key objective of our Wellness for All programme is to provide a psychological safe space where conversations around wellbeing form part of the normal open and everyday conversations that happen at SUEZ. Whilst manager support is important, peer support is much more powerful.

Working collaboratively with the Health and Safety team we began by reviewing the roles of Health and Safety representatives to incorporate wellbeing. At the same time, we carried out an audit to ensure that all of our representatives had taken part in First Aid for Mental Health Awareness training (delivered by our wellbeing partner, Goldentree CIC).

At regional Health and Safety meetings we presented our initiative, explaining the clear link between wellbeing, health, and safety. The new Health, Safety and Wellbeing representatives came into being in early May 2021, at the same time that 'wellbeing' was added to the fixed agenda at monthly site meetings and quarterly forums lead by our Regional Health and Safety Managers. We renamed the Health and Safety newsletter and added a Wellbeing feature, which gave us a vehicle to talk about wellbeing as part of health and safety. We know that poor wellbeing can be a distraction and potentially impact on safety, and there is now a clear understanding of why it's on meeting agendas and is regarded as a valuable topic for discussion. Wellbeing conversations have become the norm.

Bi-monthly Wellbeing Toolbox talks were created, hard copy as well as PowerPoint versions, which allowed us to embed short 5-minute videos from some of the experts we work with on our Wellness for All programme. Topics we have covered include: Stress and Anxiety, Five Ways to Wellbeing and Resilience. This has now evolved further into 'huddle cards' which contain QR codes to access videos via phones and encourage wellbeing discussions.

5. Measure impact and act

There is a need for better evaluation of workplace wellbeing programmes. Not only initial uptake and impact, but, where possible, sustained improvements in outcome measures, such as wellbeing, engagement and productivity, once participation in programmes ends. Assessing this 'sustainability factor' is key to ensuring that impact from any given intervention is long-lasting, and, therefore, worth the investment. While there is no standard method, it can be useful to consider both short- and long-term health and wellbeing impact (e.g., stress/mental health/sleep/fatigue/smoking) and to explore the association between health and wellbeing status and outcomes that are important to the business, such as safety incidents quality, sickness absence, talent attraction and retention, productivity, and engagement. Measuring objective as well as subjective data and including both leading and lagging measures will help assess impact in robust ways. Just as important as measuring impact is acting on the results to optimise investments made. At Serco, for instance, measures include the percentage of managers that have completed available training, company survey indicators of trust and psychological safety, sickness absence, health-related claims and EAP usage. Regularly reporting effectiveness and impact to senior leaders is good practice, as in the following example from the NHS:

> **Wrightington Wigan and Leigh Teaching Hospitals NHS Foundation Trust – Exec reporting on data and impact.**
>
> **Zoe Garnett – Staff Wellbeing Manager**
>
> To give the Executive Board Members assurances that the wellbeing service is fit for purpose and providing return on investment, we are required to submit quarterly reports to our People Committee. The report highlights wellbeing activity. The impact of this activity includes sickness absence data (in month vs baseline vs projected) and any outcomes from interventions such as the Mindful Living programme or clinical psychological support, and any risks or mitigations.

The following example, from UK Policing, highlights the importance of taking a data-driven approach to inform interventions, assess impact and influence leadership to prioritise employee health and wellbeing, through demonstrating value. It also emphasises the strong focus, within UK Policing, on employee sentiment.

UK Policing – The Covid pressure test.

UK National Police Wellbeing Service (NPWS) – Andy Rhodes and Ian Hesketh.

Policing has played a vital and often-contentious role in the national response to Covid-19. By tracking sickness, PPE usage, infection and isolation rates across all 43 forces alongside new data such as 'confidence in PPE' and 'attitudes to PPE' we have been able to provide the Gold group (established to co-ordinate the response to Covid-19) with a well-informed sense of how the workforce are feeling. This is a new experience for many senior leaders, who inevitably will have lots of competing priorities when dealing with a prolonged crisis. Of course, this trust extended to the public, who were largely compliant in the face of a fast-moving and unprecedented challenge of personal restrictions on their lives in all realms. Covid-19 tested our commitment to *'walk the talk'* under pressure. Our national survey spanned the 2020 Covid-19 period and provided us with the answer. *'Feeling valued by my line manager'* and *'my organisation'* actually increased over 2020, as well as other positive indicators such as improved sleep and improved psychological detachment. We acknowledge that although this had improved there are still worryingly high levels of sleep disruption.

We find two types of leaders when it comes down to stepping up to their responsibility for wellbeing. Many leaders truly believe it is the right thing to do – their hearts are in it and so they just need help working out what to do. Some leaders want more proof and need convincing of the return on investment (ROI) or the risk/benefits; they are ruled by their heads. Our influencing strategy addresses both types of leadership approach. We have deduced that data is quite often our most powerful tool when seeking to engage and influence 'head' leaders. Our quest for accurate ROI modelling – or, to put it another way, health economics – goes on.

In summary, embedding these five key fundamental approaches will ensure that all health and wellbeing efforts are fully realised.

ACTIONS

1. Regularly communicate at an enterprise-wide level the importance of wellbeing and resources available, to improve awareness and uptake.
2. Take a data-driven approach, to identify employee needs, to decide which solutions to deploy and to assess impact of interventions.
3. Solicit employee 'voice of the customer' to identify employee needs, co-create solutions and to seek their feedback on usefulness of EH&W resources available, regularly.
4. Ensure available EH&W resources are relevant to the needs of the employee population, culturally appropriate, easy to engage with and adaptable, to meet the changing needs of the employee population.
5. Leverage digitalisation to improve awareness and reach and look for opportunities to integrate efforts with partners in other functions, to enhance reach and impact.
6. Harness employee passion in EH&W to create EH&W ambassadors and champions. Consider creating peer-peer support networks, to support each other on a day-to-day basis. adequate training and ongoing supervision must be provided.
7. Source trained and experienced experts in occupational health and wellbeing, who deeply understand the impact of work on health and health on work and will take an evidence based, data-driven approach.
8. Measure and review the usage of EH&W services, perceived value and their impact, and adapt your approach accordingly, in a data-informed way.

REFERENCES

Blake, H., Bermingham, F., Johnson, G., & Tabner, A. (2020). Mitigating the psychological impact of COVID-19 on healthcare workers: A digital learning package. *International Journal of Environmental Research and Public Health*, *17*(9), 2997.

Coe, R., Enomoto, K., Gupta, A., & Lewis, R. (2020). *National employer survey reveals behavioral health in a COVID-19 era as a major concern.* McKinsey & Company. https://www.mckinsey.com/industries/healthcare/our-insights/national-employer-survey-reveals-behavioral-health-in-a-covid-19-era-as-a-major-concern#/

Gnanapragasam, S.N., Tinch-Taylor, R., Scott, H.R., Hegarty, S., Souliou, E., Bhundia, R., … & Wessely, S. (2023). Multicentre, England-wide randomised controlled trial of the 'Foundations' smartphone application in improving mental health and well-being in a healthcare worker population. *The British Journal of Psychiatry, 222*(2), 58–66.

Lamb, D., Gnanapragasam, S., Greenberg, N., Bhundia, R., Carr, E., Hotopf, M., … & Wessely, S. (2021). Psychosocial impact of the COVID-19 pandemic on 4378 UK healthcare workers and ancillary staff: Initial baseline data from a cohort study collected during the first wave of the pandemic. *Occupational and Environmental Medicine, 78*(11), 801–808.

Shah, W., Hillman, T., Playford, E.D., & Hishmeh, L. (2021). Managing the long term effects of covid-19: Summary of NICE, SIGN, and RCGP rapid guideline. *BMJ, 372.*

Shanafelt, T., Ripp, J., & Trockel, M. (2020). Understanding and addressing sources of anxiety among health care professionals during the COVID-19 pandemic. *JAMA, 323*(21), 2133–2134.

INDEX